Grandmother's House

American Places of the Heart

Sea Island Yankee
by Clyde Bresee

*The Blessed Town: Oxford, Georgia, at the Turn
of the Century*
by Polly Stone Buck

Grandmother's House
by Frances Clausen Chapman

American Places of the Heart

Grandmother's House

∵ ∵ ∵

Frances Clausen Chapman

with illustrations by
Robert Alden Rubin

Algonquin Books of Chapel Hill
1987

published by

Algonquin Books of Chapel Hill
Post Office Box 2225
Chapel Hill, North Carolina 27515-2225

in association with

Taylor Publishing Company
1550 West Mockingbird Lane
Dallas, Texas 75235

Illustrations by Robert Alden Rubin

LIBRARY OF CONGRESS CATALOGING-IN-PUBLICATION DATA

Chapman, Frances Clausen, 1920–
Grandmother's house.
(American places of the heart)
I. Title.   II. Series.
PS3553.H28G7   1987   813'.54   87-11354
ISBN 0-912697-62-8

In recounting from memory one faces the question of what was "real" and what was imagined.

But remembering is often a creative process. We remember what *was* as what, in our view, *could* have been.

The sense of place and persons in this account is based on the reality of memory.

In no Atchison phone book of any date can one find the names of the persons here mentioned.

—F. C. C.
December 1986

Contents

Undertow

People said about them—once I heard that people talked about them at all—overheard, really, for it was my Grandmother Henley telling my mother—people said that the two of them sat in the upstairs front window of the red brick house and stared at the street all day. They were so immobile that they looked as if they were etched on glass, people said.

I wanted to see that, but I never did. Whenever I passed the house on Fourth Street, after I knew it was theirs, I'd look at that upstairs window. But I never saw them. I never saw anything.

Even that day that I went up to the Paulsen house. When I didn't know that I meant to.

I was on Fourth Street . . .
I was in front of the steps leading from the sidewalk to the porch . . .
I paused, and then I mounted the steps.
I rang the bell and waited. Beyond the curtained front door, the house seemed to come alert and then to wait, too. I had the feeling of being seen. Then a figure moved behind the door, and a finger pushed the starched gauzy curtain an inch aside . . .

Somewhere in that house, I knew, was the grandmother I had never seen.

My Other Grandmother.

Grandmother's House

I

Grandmother's House

Sometimes I dream about the houses I've lived in. No, not really *about* them. They are the background for the action of my dreams, and I hardly notice them. Except for Grandmother Henley's house. That is a character in itself, an emotional force in my dream.

I am usually going through the house, trying to learn every detail, to hold it all in my mind so that it will always be mine. It is desperately important that I know just what kind of chair is in the living room. Sometimes, as I make my way through the rooms, I cry.

As I first knew it, the exterior of Grandmother Henley's house was clapboard, painted barn red. But later, sometime still in the twenties, I suppose, the house was dressed up and modernized with a covering of tan stucco and chocolate trim. This change caused a feeling of up-to-dateness and self-congratulation for my grandparents and was maintained for the next thirty or so years. It was my uncle's wife who suggested that the house be painted green to harmonize with the roof, pointing out that my grandfather was now confined to his bedroom and would never see the difference. A new color scheme would make the house more salable once he died, she said. This suggestion caused a fracas between her and my mother, as most of her attitudes did.

The house had been planned by my grandfather and was built on one end of my great-grandparents' grounds. My uncle told me once that it was where the mule corral used to be. My great-grandfather had owned mule teams for overland shipping to Denver until the railroad—the Atchison, Topeka, and Santa Fe—had made this business unprofitable, and he had concentrated on his flour mill.

Except for the first year of her marriage, while the house was under construction, my grandmother lived all of her life on the same street. She did not remember the year away with pleasure. In winter the rented house was so cold that the scrub water froze on the kitchen floor, and the walls were so thin that when my grandfather caught cold, Grandmother sent him outdoors to cough and blow his nose so that the noise would not wake the baby, my mother.

Sometime near 1890 the house was ready, and the family moved to the address which I always associated with my grandparents: 1021 North Third Street, Atchison, Kansas. There they lived for the remainder of the sixty-year-long marriage, and there my grandfather died at ninety-two.

By the time I knew it, the front walk leading from the sidewalk to the porch steps and curving around the side of the house had been paved with concrete. But once out of sight of those approaching the front, the walk changed back into striated brick, laid in a herringbone pattern. This was much more fun to walk on because you could fit your feet onto the bricks and waddle along, duck-fashion, with your heels touching, or pigeon-toeing it, depending on which direction you headed. The brick path continued past the back porch, which was really on the side of the house, and curved around to the basement door. Then it became a wood-plank walk leading, with a step or two at the terrace, down past the chicken house (still red clapboard; nobody ever thought to stucco it over) to the alley gate.

I liked the chicken house, but I didn't like the chickens. They were excitable, unpredictable things that flopped in the air with a great squawking when Grandmother urged them off their nests. I disliked the possibility of being brushed by their awkward wings, and I didn't like putting my hand into the warm nest to feel around for the egg. I was always braced to pull my hand out of the repellent, dark straw at first contact with those wet, warm chicken droppings I was sure I would find. I thought that the two-room chicken house would be a good playhouse, but by the time the chickens were no longer there, I had lost interest in such things, or felt I shouldn't show it. Once I decided that I would like to watch Grandfather kill the chicken for Sunday dinner. There was a discreet conference between Mother and Grandmother to decide whether such exposure would be upsetting, and for some reason I was allowed to attend the execution. I felt somehow that Grandfather was more loath to have me than they to permit me, but he had a way of stoically accepting the inevitable. In his harsh pepper-and-salt suit (it always scratched when you sat on his lap), elbows and knees akimbo, he brought the hatchet above his head and then down on the chicken skewered on the old stump. Of course I was shocked by the blood and the flopping creature, though I don't recall losing my appetite for fried chicken. But it was Grandfather I noticed most. I realized with some surprise that, Pennsylvania farm boy though he had been, he did not take this assignment calmly, had, in fact, to force himself to do something which repelled his sensitive nature. But, good Presbyterian that he was, he roused himself to the duty to which his man's role compelled him. I came away having learned as much about my grandfather as about chicken killing.

Beyond the chicken house, the plank walk ended at the gate into the alley. You could cut up the alley which led behind my great-grandmother's house and come out on the street where stood the garage in which Grandfather kept his succession of Hudsons. Be-

Grandmother's House

fore it was a garage, it had been Great-grandmother's stable, and "the boys," Grandmother's brothers, had kept their horses there. Majors, the yard man, lived upstairs. The stairs went up from inside the dirt-floored garage. Mother said I shouldn't go up there.

The concrete front walk (perhaps it was part of the modernizing at the time of the stucco) led to the steps at the center of the front porch. It was a wonderful porch. One side of it swept out in a huge half circle with built-in curved seats against the inner side of the balustrade and window boxes of geraniums on the railings. The big wooden swing that Uncle Graham had built and stained when he took manual training in high school was suspended from the ceiling. (Although my mother had attended CPS, the private college preparatory school founded by two Wellesley graduates, by the time my uncle came along, Grandfather was on the school board and led the effort to build a new high school, so my uncle attended the public high school.) The swing was bigger by half than an ordinary swing, and it was marvelous to play on. You could stand on the arms, holding on to the heavy, rusty chains that stretched in a V to the varnished ceiling, and you could make the swing move sideways very rapidly. Sometimes when your boat or train was going very fast, it would hit the wooden seat on one side or crash into a corner of the wall on the other. You were warned about that; there was always the danger of gouging a piece out of the stucco. In the summer cretonne-covered pads were tied on the seat and back of the swing, and the dark, varnished wicker furniture was brought out. On hot summer afternoons, friends of Mother's and Grandmother's came to call, and we sat there on the porch, drinking lemonade and eating cake. I passed the cake.

Eventually it was decided that Grandfather should have protection against mosquitoes as he relaxed on the porch after dinner. To screen in the whole porch seemed too much, so the straight part, beginning on the other side of the steps, was enclosed, to make a rectangular box. The dark wicker couch and several high-backed wicker chairs and a table were placed there.

"Go out and sit with Grandfather," I would be told when he settled down after dinner.

"Hello, Topsy," he would greet me, and we would sit together and watch the stately movement of the occasional traffic on the broad, tree-shaded street before us. Grandfather would identify the passersby, sometimes calling out to one of the Riley boys.

"Hello, Tom!"

"Hello, Mr. Henley." It was always said respectfully.

"Going to be this hot for the game Friday?"

"I sure hope not, Mr. Henley." Grandfather would chuckle.

The Rileys lived in one of the little houses down the street, an

unending number of boys. They all played baseball at St. Bene-
dict's, and then they became priests. I would go with Grandfather
to watch the games at the college and hear Grandfather exchange
greetings. "Hello, Mr. Henley," respectfully, and "Hello, Father"—
or "Tom," if the priest was just one of the Riley boys not too
recently grown up. Grandfather was the only non-Catholic asked
to sit on the platform for formal events at the college. The family
spoke of the honor proudly, because it proved how tolerant Grandfather was. I don't recall Grandfather ever saying anything about
it.

Callers came to the screened porch in the evening, too. A big
slow car would lumber to the curb and "the girls" would get out.
Grandfather immediately became jocular as Miss Effie, with the
hearing aid, and Miss Mame, with the white hair, came laughing
and chattering up the walk. Miss Mame and Miss Effie lived together in Miss Effie's big white house set back in the trees several
streets over. Miss Mame drove Miss Effie's car and talked all the
time. She wore tight boucle knit suits in bright blues and pinks.
Miss Effie was related to Lieutenant Rowan, who carried the message to General Garcia during the Spanish-American War. The
lieutenant's wife and his daughter Elizabeth had come to Atchison
to stay during that time, and Mother and Elizabeth played together
while Lieutenant Rowan carried the message to Garcia.

Mother said she could remember Grandfather coming home for
the noon meal and calling upstairs to Grandmother,

"We're at war with Spain!"

But the only change the war made in her life was the chance to
play with Elizabeth Rowan in Miss Effie's big white house.

Sometimes when Grandfather and I were sitting on the front
porch, Amy and Ann came. They were mother's unmarried friends
who were available for bridge or trips to St. Joe for lunch. Amy

was Catholic and lived with her deaf mother over on Seventh Street within walking distance of the church. She made cookies she called "Amy's Almond Aces" and packaged in cans with the name on them. Ann was Ann Spiegel and kind of a relative. At least she was a cousin of someone I called Uncle Henry Spiegel because years ago he had been married to a relative of my father's. I think Ann also had a widowed mother living with her for a long time but went cheerfully on, living in a large house with a servant or two coming in after her mother's death. Houses in Atchison formed the immutability and the continuity in a person's life. You just went on living in your house until you died. Whoever was the last survivor was the last man out, and only then did houses change families.

The last time I sat with Grandfather on the front porch was the summer that my second baby was ten months old. We had driven to Atchison to let Grandmother and Grandfather see the children. ("Oh, tomorrow I won't have a baby to love," Grandmother said on the last day of our visit.) Grandfather, the baby, and I sat on the swing. The baby had been crawling and was happily grimy. I tried to wipe his face, and he ducked his head.

"For generations," reflected Grandfather, "mothers have been washing boys' faces—and boys have been resisting."

Musing, we rocked silently, in and out of the time we occupied. Back to memories of Grandfather's mother, wiping the faces of her three resisting boys. Forward to my baby, here to my repeating the pattern with him. Back and forth, back and forth.

Remember this, remember this, I thought then. Hold on to the hot breeze, the bright geraniums in their boxes, the comfortable sense of the ordered day, the ordered life with immutable times for meals, for naps. The shared silence . . .

The ordered life would soon shatter. Grandmother would be

carried, unconscious, from her sunny yellow-flowered bedroom to the alien hospital on the hill. Grandfather, helpless, would sit by her bed.

"Hold her hand, Mr. Henley," said the nurse. "She'll know you're there, even if she can't speak." He fumbled for her hand.

"I tried to take care of her," he cried on the way to the cemetery. "I promised when we got married that I'd take care of her." The promise was sixty years old.

Then, bereft of companion and purpose, a suddenly old man would give up the porch, the leather chair in the library, the meals at the dining room table. Swollen-legged, sighing, bewildered, he would be helped from the massive bed to his chair and spend his days in his room. Sometimes in warm weather he would be bundled up for a ride. As he faltered down the porch steps, holding the rail, he would pause. "Are you going to leave Mrs. Henley all alone in there?"

"Mrs. Henley's dead, Mr. Henley."

"Oh." A sigh of renewed pain . . .

It hasn't happened. Not yet. Back and forth. Back and forth. The swing creaks.

There will never be another time.

2

Before

My great-grandmother Graham lived in a log cabin when she was a little girl. She died at eighty-two, peacefully asleep in bed in her big stone house with the ballroom on the third floor. Her progression in living accommodations told some of the story of the country during the nineteenth century. Many a family went from hardscrabble to a fortune in one lifetime.

I don't know if the log cabin was a home of long duration or temporary quarters while the family built something better. Great-grandmother's was the third family in Atchison, whatever Atchison was at the time. Her father owned the first hotel in town. She was the one who told her children about living in the cabin. She didn't like the white part of a fried egg, but her mother said she had to sit at the table until her egg was all gone. So when her mother wasn't looking, Great-grandmother poked the egg white through the chinks in the cabin wall to the chickens pecking in the dirt outside. She thought it funny that the chickens turned into cannibals, eating their own eggs. It was a joke that she couldn't share until she was grown up. My mother, in telling me the story, said that wasn't a nice thing to do, fooling your mother like that. After all, mothers only did what was best for you.

But then, Mother said, except for my grandmother the Grahams weren't as "fine" as the Henleys. Mother always said that she herself was more Henley than Graham, whereas her brother Graham was more Graham than Henley.

Certainly their grandfather Graham made a companion of my uncle Graham when he was a small boy. My uncle said that his grandfather would take him downtown in Atchison and would let my uncle hold the reins of the old horse, Daddy, while his grandfather passed the time of day with his cronies along Commercial Street. Edward Graham was well known in the town. As a boat captain on the Missouri River he decided to settle in Atchison after his boat, the *J.P. Ransom*, had burned and sunk. My uncle said that the fire started because his grandfather had been cheap and bought green wood which didn't burn right and caused the boiler to explode. He said that the passengers all dove overboard and swam for the Missouri side, but that Great-grandfather went into all of the cabins and collected all of the money and valuables, and then *he* jumped over and swam for the Kansas side. My uncle said that Great-grandfather nearly drowned, he was so weighted down. And that, said my uncle, was how his grandfather had the money to buy into the flour mill. First he went into partnership with Mr. Moore, who owned the mill, which became known as Graham and Moore. Then he bought out Mr. Moore and made the mill into the Graham Milling Company, home of Graham's Certified Flours. Mother said she never heard that story about the money and how her grandfather got it, and that Graham must be making it all up. Still, she said, the Grahams weren't as fine as the Henleys. . . .

Great-grandfather liked making money, and he liked talking to people. Much traffic went through Atchison into the newly expanding West, and for a time Great-grandfather was in the overland shipping business. Eventually, the Atchison, Topeka and Santa Fe Railroad was able to do the job better. No matter, the mill was growing, and he was becoming part of the political life of the town.

He ran for alderman and was elected, and then he was mayor of Atchison for three terms. But my uncle Graham said his grandfather didn't really like to work too hard. I guess he had done that for a long time, leaving home in Pennsylvania at fourteen after his mother's death and his father's remarriage. That was when he began to know the rivers, shipping on first as a cabin boy and finally making his way out West to ownership of his own boat.

Atchison had sprung into being almost full blown as a commercial center in the 1850s. Its position on the river gave it advantages for shipping, and it was a center for travelers early. Grandmother's grandfather had opened the first hotel in town the year before Atchison was incorporated as a town in 1855.

The railroad and telegraph entered Atchison almost simultaneously. In June of 1855 Atchison was selected by a number of Salt Lake freighters as their outfitting and starting point on the Missouri River. Immense traffic poured through Atchison, heading west. The city became the eastern terminus of the Great Overland Stage Line, said to be the longest single route in the world. Even before that time, the locality was recognized as a splendid point of departure for the "interior," being twelve miles further west than any other landing on the river.

My uncle Graham said that when he would be sitting in the buggy with his grandfather, holding old Daddy's reins that way, my grandmother and Great-grandmother Graham would be across the street in their carriage, attending to the marketing. They didn't go into the stores. That wasn't necessary. The grocer would come out to the carriage and present a head of cauliflower or whatever was wanted for their inspection. Like as not they would wave it away as inferior, and the grocer would scurry back into the shop to return with another offering. They would never acknowledge the presence across the street of the little boy and the man laughing so heartily with the barber or the poolhall proprietor. But when they came home, Great-grandmother would "speak to" her husband about exposing Graham to heavens knew what kind of rough-talk. "Oh, the boy has to learn about life," would be the response. Nothing changed.

Great-grandfather had four sons to carry on the mill, but not all of them did. Uncle Will, the eldest, went into the business and became president after his father's death. But Ed, the namesake of his father, wanted to be a doctor. That was something that Great-grandfather didn't approve. But Ed went off to New York to study medicine anyway, and Grandmother and Great-grandmother sent him money because his father wouldn't. When my grandparents married, Ed painted them a picture of a street in Paris (which he had not yet seen) for a wedding present because he couldn't afford to buy anything. The picture hung in the front room of my grandparents' house over the player piano until Grandmother finally gave the piano to the Presbyterian Church for the Sunday School room. After that it didn't hang over anything, but it still stayed on the wall in the front room. I don't know what my mother did with it when she dismantled the house after my grandparents' death. The painting was a hideous chromo with a peculiar perspective.

When Uncle Will died, Uncle Wesley stepped in as president of the mill. He also moved into Great-grandmother's house after she died and he was divorced. He was president for only about seven years before his death. Grandmother had him laid out on the bed in the Blue Bedroom before they buried him in the family plot in the cemetery where I used to play on Sunday afternoons while Grandmother arranged fresh flowers in the green tin vases sunk at the head of each grave.

Of course, there was Uncle Elwood, the youngest, but he never worked at anything. Great-grandmother had spoiled him. I met

Before

him only once, even though I knew Aunt Louisa, who had divorced
him, and their daughter, Eloise, Mother's cousin, and Eloise's son,
Rex, who was my age. Grandmother didn't approve of Elwood
much. Even in her girlhood diary she wrote accounts of his mis-
demeanors. "Elwood set the chip box on fire. It caught the window
and burnt to the ceiling." The one time I saw him was almost by
accident. He was delivering eggs to Grandmother. By this time he
lived on a farm and was married to a woman "much younger,"
Grandmother said. When he brought the eggs, Grandmother
called down to me and said, "The money is in my black purse on
the hall table," and didn't come downstairs or even call hello to
him.

We stood and talked, being extra friendly to each other because
we were getting acquainted. He was small, as most of the Grahams
were, and had the snowy, wavy hair that Grandmother had and
that I remembered as Great-grandmother's. Then, feeling a little
awkward about it, I counted out the change from Grandmother's
purse, put it in his hand, and he smiled and thanked me. He didn't
know his grandson Rex as well as I did, so we couldn't talk about
him, and he left quickly after he got the money.

After Uncle Wes died, my uncle Graham became president of
the mill. Actually, he was the one who served longest in that ca-
pacity. Because he was named for his grandfather—Edward Graham Henley was his full name—and had started as a small boy to
learn about life from him, that's probably the way things should
have been.

It's a good thing that Great-grandfather liked to make money,
because Great-grandmother liked to spend it, especially after he
died. I guess she was entitled to enjoy it at that. Eighteen when
she married, she was mother to my grandmother nine months later.
The four boys came along after that. Grandmother's girlhood journal refers repeatedly to diphtheria and to children in the town

dying, but despite the sore throats that she reports, she and her brothers all survived. She refers to "Ma" being sick a lot too, or "Ma and I" putting up cherries or making cider or jellies or doing the work because "the girl" left.

"Work, work, work," Grandmother exploded in her journal. "Anyone reading this journal would think I hated to work. True it is. I do not like to wash dishes and such." As the eldest child and only daughter, Grandmother was expected to share domestic responsibilities. Although she may have felt rebellious sometimes, she was also contrite at her own inadequacies:

> I did not get up very early this morning. (about half past 6) got a scolding. nothing unusual I am so helter Skelter about every thing ... Ma has a terrible head ache. the least noise hurts her head. I drop a great many things.

Yet, for the times and the town she must have led a life of relative privilege. She speaks of music lessons, of playing the organ in church ("and made a fool of myself as Will said," quoting her brother's remark) and of going to school at Mrs. Monroe's, instead of "the public." Later she went off for a year at Monticello, a young ladies' seminary in Alton, Illinois.

So life was probably as comfortable for the Graham family as for anyone in Atchison. Even so, there was much for the women to do. Great-grandmother evidently turned her hand competently to whatever was needed, whether it was putting out Elwood's fire in the chip box ("but for Ma's thoughtfulness, the house would have burnt down"), washing the family poodle after she had seen to the children's Saturday night baths, or delivering her own grandson, my uncle Graham. The last accomplishment hadn't been planned that way. Grandmother was laboring at home, as everyone in Atchison did in those days, with her brother Edward, now a doctor, checking on her. He decided that the time hadn't come yet, so he went downtown for a while. Whereupon, Uncle Graham arrived, with Grandmother and Great-grandmother doing what was necessary between them. Shortly afterwards, Grandfather arrived home for noonday dinner. Great-grandmother, standing at the head of the stairs announced,

"You have a son."

"No!" said Grandfather, although he could not have been totally surprised.

"*Yes!*" mocked Great-grandmother, who never felt much love for the male sex just after an experience with childbirth.

Mother, then four years old, had been dispatched next door to Great-grandmother's house to wait out the event, although she had no idea what was happening. She said that when she came home and saw that baby in bed with her mother, she wanted to get him out.

Great-grandfather was nearly twelve years senior to his wife. When he died, of a "tobacco heart" it was said, Great-grandmother was fifty-six years old. She lived on in good health, tyrannizing over the entire family for another twenty-six years, dying on the anniversary of her husband's death. I never knew how much she cared for him. Grandmother used to say she realized too late that her father was hungry for affection. She said her mother was afraid to be affectionate with him for fear of "arousing" him. Great-grandmother lived on in the big house, spending money and having her own way. Later on, she required my grandparents and their family to move in with her for one year, although they lived just next door, and Great-grandfather had been dead for years. So they rented their house out to some bachelors, and Grandmother mourned at the sight of those men putting their feet on the porch railing of her house.

My parents were embarked on their long engagement then. As

Great-grandmother Graham

I learned later, both from things Mother told me and from the diaries and letters which I read after my parents' deaths, it was not a uniformly happy time. The reasons, the unresolvable problems, became a part of my knowledge as I grew older.

I heard first of the times when my father was becoming an accepted part of Mother's family. For a long time I didn't wonder whether Mother was becoming close to my father's mother and sister.

My father sometimes drove the White steamer car which Great-grandmother had bought, the first such car in Atchison. One of those Sunday drives took the family up along the river bluffs. Rounding a bend, they faced a farmer driving a team of horses. The horses, unused to any vehicle more sophisticated than the wagon they pulled, shied and leaped in terror over the side of the bluff. Setting the brake, my father ran to look over the cliff's edge, expecting to see a scene of carnage. Instead, he saw the farmer, still seated in the wagon, still holding the reins. He looked up at my father, wagged his head toward the struggling horses, and said, "Well—I didn't think they'd do that."

One evening, bringing Mother home to Great-grandmother's house late, my father discovered that the family was asleep, the house was locked, and Mother had no key. Reluctant to ring the bell (it *was* late) he reconnoitered until he found an open window in the pantry. He hoisted himself over the sill and dropped to the floor inside—directly into a basket of eggs.

When Great-grandmother got it into her head to go to Alaska, she took Mother along. They took a steamship from the West Coast. Although they were late and arrived as the last whistle blew, Great-grandmother couldn't—or wouldn't—hurry. Mother ran ahead and stood on the gangplank so it couldn't be pulled up until they were aboard. I don't know whether that was her idea or Great-grandmother's.

During World War I, wheat, among other commodities, was in short supply, and allotments to individuals were limited. Great-grandmother hoarded wheat in the third-floor ballroom until her cache was discovered and she had to pay a fine. She was indignant. After all, they owned the mill. What difference whether the wheat was stored in the grain elevator or at home?

All of those events happened before I knew Great-grandmother. Actually, I have only two memories of her, although when I was warned to be careful not to break the elephant ears growing in the round bed astride the unseen boundary line between her house and Grandmother's, I always felt that it was Great-grandmother who would be displeased, not Grandmother. Grandmother was willing to have me play hide-and-seek among the broad-leaved plants, but she still did things the way her mother wanted. Her one show of independence was about the bread. Great-grandmother never allowed bread to be cut when it was hot from the oven. While Grandmother was growing up she announced that when *she* had her own home, she would let anyone who wished cut a slice of hot bread. And she did, rather defiantly.

Perhaps Grandmother felt that her attempts to defy her mother during her youth had been disastrous. She had wanted to have her ears pierced for earrings as her friends were doing. Great-grandmother said no, so Grandmother and a friend decided to do the job secretly. They went into the kitchen. Grandmother bent over the kitchen table and rested her ear lobe on a bar of soap. The friend stabbed her lobe with an ice pick, but, on seeing the blood, ran screaming from the room, leaving Grandmother pinned to the bar of soap *and* the kitchen table. Of course, it was her mother who discovered and liberated her. In telling me about it later, Grandmother added that her mother said as long as one ear was pierced, she might as well have the other one done. She could show me the scars where the holes had filled up.

Events like that may have had something to do with Grandmother's continual desire to please her mother. I recall Grandmother leading me up the hill to where Great-grandmother, seated on her front porch, held court.

I was up from my nap, freshly dressed, my hair having been brushed in curls around Grandmother's finger. Those fingers as she held my hand were tense. I had the vague sense, though I could not have defined it then, that Grandmother was nervous. She was presenting me for Great-grandmother's approval, which was never a certainty.

Great-grandmother seemed vast and white. Her hair was piled high on her head like meringue, and her white dress was all leg-o'-mutton sleeves and full skirts to the porch floor. I looked dubiously at those skirts. Grandmother told me that when she and her brothers were small and played hiding games, they sometimes hid under their mother's skirts. How did they dare? Great-grandmother didn't seem to me to be one for a game. I thought I would prefer the elephant ears.

She must have said something, but I don't recall a word or that she touched me. She inclined her head royally in a nod of acceptance, and my presentation at court was successfully over.

My only other memory of Great-grandmother was of a hot summer day when I was playing outside her house with Sarah Margaret, Uncle Wesley's daughter. Sarah Margaret had been named for Great-grandmother, at least the Margaret part. Great-grandmother had been Margaret Eaton, and then she was Margaret Eaton Graham after she married Great-grandfather. The marvelous thing was that her initials spelled her nickname Meg. Because of having part of Great-grandmother's name, Sarah Margaret was always called the whole thing, at least until Great-grandmother died. Then she became Peggy, and I heard later that when she went away to New York she called herself Margo.

That summer Sarah Margaret was a "big girl," probably eight or nine years old to my three-and-a-half. She had on a red dotted-swiss dress with white dots, and I told her timidly and a little proudly that at home I had a dress of the same material. I thought that having a dress like Sarah Margaret's would make me seem more grown up, but Sarah Margaret didn't seem to think so.

Sarah Margaret, being the elder, decided what we should play. She suggested what seemed to me a rather pointless game of running in opposite directions around the house. I complied and plodded, panting, as she directed. Sarah Margaret cheated. I don't know just how, but she did cheat. I felt outraged, but said nothing until Mother put me to bed that night, and I told her that Sarah Margaret wasn't honest. Mother agreed that she had been wrong.

Before we started our game, Sarah Margaret asked me if I wanted a drink of water. I said no. She sternly asked if I was sure. I said I was. I really hadn't thought about the possibility until she suggested it. But as we circled the house in the hot sun, I began to realize that I did want a drink, very much. The next time I passed Sarah Margaret I told her so. She reminded me that she had offered me my chance and that I had turned it down. Then, sighing, she led me into the house and told Great-grandmother just how trying I was. Great-grandmother glided silently across the floor of the darkened dining room, its shades drawn against the heat. She reached down a glass from the top shelf of the built-in cupboard while I watched with dry lips. She filled the glass from the sweating cut-crystal pitcher on the tea cart and handed it to me. I wondered whether she thought I was a very bad girl, but she said nothing. Sarah Margaret and she watched as I gulped down the water, spilling some on my chin. Then I went out to run around the house some more.

Most people treated Great-grandmother with frightened respect. The only person who could get her to see reason was my grandfather Henley.

Hiram Hamilton Henley, named for his father, who had added the Hamilton to his own name out of admiration for Alexander Hamilton, grew up on a farm outside of Uniontown, Pennsylvania. He told me how, as a boy, he had stood by the side of a dusty road and watched Sherman's troops returning from the South, driving stolen cattle before them.

He attended "Mercantile College" and a Normal School and later taught school. His father, a Quaker who evidently epitomized at least the latter part of the saying about Quakers: "They came to do good and stayed to do well," had traversed the country for years on various projects. My uncle Graham told me, "He'd come home just long enough to get Grandma pregnant, and then he'd take off again."

In his travels he acquired interests in a Wyoming sheep ranch and in several banks. When my grandfather turned twenty-one, his father asked him, "Do you want to go into the bank here in Uniontown or the one in Atchison?"

As my uncle Graham said, "Trust Father. He chose the wrong bank."

He chose to come west, to Atchison.

The bank position in Uniontown came, by default, to his next brother, who became the family millionaire. Uncle Edgar was the one with the winter home in Florida and the private railroad car. When he sometimes visited us in our St. Louis home during my childhood, he seemed, even to me, a rather shy, sweet man, a dispenser of fabulous gifts which he commissioned my mother to pick out for me. One was a pale green crepe de chine dress with smocking and pink rosebuds. I wore it even after I outgrew it. But just as interesting as the gifts was the special gluten bread which Uncle Edgar, a diabetic, carried with him. He let me eat some of it with him at dinner.

The West in the late nineteenth century was flourishing, but so was lawlessness. Jesse James and his gang roamed the countryside just across the Missouri River. There was the time when a stranger was observed loitering across from the Atchison bank. Was he a lookout for the James boys, scouting their next strike? The sheriff ran him off, but the townspeople were left wary of unfamiliar persons who lingered too long without known business.

When I was small, Grandfather showed me a framed picture which he had of Jesse James. Jesse was up on a chair, hanging a picture for his wife, Grandfather explained. And that was when someone outside shot him in the back. The whole episode introduced some delicate moral points for Grandfather. It was wrong to shoot someone in the back; it was cowardly. And Jesse was in the midst of doing a good, loving deed. But he had been a bad man. Maybe he deserved to die, but not that way.... I thought that Grandfather began to regret that he had ever shown me the picture.

Grandfather came west for good reasons. He told me, "I was just a little country boy when I came to Atchison. I had never seen street lights before."

By the time that Grandfather came to Atchison in 1880, there had been a generation to accumulate and enjoy the wealth created by the westward movement. Atchison people had begun to travel into the greater world which expanded their tastes and desires. And they had begun to build mansions.

One such mansion was built by my great-grandparents Graham. As a young man, new in town, Grandfather was brought to call on the Grahams. At the conclusion of his visit, Great-grandmother said graciously, "Come see us again, Mr. Henley." A year later he returned. At the end of *that* visit, Great-grandmother said, "Mr. Henley, when you came before, I asked you to come again. But if you can't come in less than a year, don't bother to come at all."

He came and courted. During the engagement period, Grandfather fell ill with something that affected his eyes, making it impossible for him to read. He lived in a rooming house at the time, and Great-grandfather Graham paid him a visit every day. It wasn't proper for my grandmother to visit a man's bedroom, so she sent daily letters by her father. Grandfather couldn't read them, and he was too private a person to want anyone to read them to him. He received each letter gladly and tucked it under his pillow. When he was well enough, he read them all at once. I can't imagine that those sessions with Great-grandfather were very comforting. After all, when my grandparents courted on the Graham front porch,

Great-grandfather was apt to call down, "If you don't want to sleep, other people do!"

After marriage to Grandmother, Grandfather soon came to be considered the dependable one in the family, and especially after Great-grandfather's death he became the peacemaker. His sound financial judgment and his sense of fair play, combined with his true respect for every human being—a legacy, perhaps, from his Quaker forebears—inspired cooperation in most persons. So he was assigned the role of persuader whenever there were difficulties in the family.

I suspect that Grandfather put up with a lot from Great-grandmother and used his persuasion skills only for major issues. I remember his saying that my grandmother "wore herself out, running up the hill to do things for her mother," so I imagine that he may have silently resented Great-grandmother's imperious disruption of his home life on many occasions.

Perhaps she was trying to be imperious at the last. Grandmother had come to visit us in Kirkwood, Missouri, to help nurse Mother after a miscarriage. In a dream, she heard her mother calling her. When she woke the next morning, Uncle Wes telephoned to say that their mother had died in her sleep.

It was then that Uncle Wes, divorced and single, moved into Great-grandmother's house, where Grandmother, out of habit, kept a careful eye on things. Once she took me to sit with Uncle Wes while he ate his solitary dinner, so that he would have company. Grandmother sat at the far end of the table, miles, it seemed to me, from Uncle Wes, who sat at the head. The long damask table cloth hung to the floor on either side of the table, making a white tunnel through which the chandelier lights glowed softly. Bare-kneed on the carpet, I crawled beneath the table from one end to the other. When I came to Uncle Wes's chair, I popped my head out from under the cloth and opened my mouth. Uncle Wes dropped a bit of celery heart into my mouth, and I crawled back to Grandmother. We repeated this procedure until Uncle Wes, looking concerned, said, "I don't have any more hearts. Is it all right if I give her plain celery?" and Grandmother nodded. I thought it strange that a grown-up had to ask permission.

Eventually, Great-grandmother's house was sold to the Harveys. I wondered if Grandmother minded having other people living in her family home, but it never seemed to bother her. She and Mother liked Grace Harvey, and Grandmother enjoyed seeing signs of more activity than had been true in recent years. Junior Harvey was about my age and was a good playmate during my visits to Atchison. I was actually in and out of Great-grandmother's house more—and more comfortably—than I had ever been before. It seemed to me a brighter and lighter place than I had remembered.

One thing was strange, though. Grace Harvey changed the front steps. When Great-grandmother was alive, the steps came off the side of the porch, aiming you towards Grandmother's house as you descended. When Great-grandmother sat on her front porch, she faced the steps, looking right down the hill to Grandmother's porch. She could see the dining room windows and those of the bedrooms on that side of the house. But Grace Harvey took those steps out and continued the balustrade around the side of the porch. She had new steps put in the center, in line with the front door. The new steps connected with a concrete walk that led to the front terrace and down some more steps to the street. It seemed to me unthinkable that someone could change something that Great-grandmother had decreed. It made a real difference.

Grandmother's house had always appeared to look respectfully up the hill at Great-grandmother's, which had seemed to maintain a sort of sideways surveillance. With the steps repositioned, the two houses turned their heads away from each other. They now stood independent, though side by side, squarely facing out to the street.

3

Beginnings

When my father and his sister Dud and their mother, my grandmother Paulsen, came to Atchison, they had no connections but Uncle Henry. Uncle Henry had been married to my grandmother's younger sister, Adelia, for whom Dud was named, but both Adelia and her baby had died, and Uncle Henry was alone. Even before my father finished law school, Uncle Henry wrote that he should consider coming to Atchison. They needed young lawyers there, he said.

Grandmother Paulsen had already moved from her home in Carrollton, Missouri, to Columbia when, just before he was sixteen, my father entered the University of Missouri. She thought he was too young to be away from home. There was no real reason to go back to Carrollton, although she had family there. Uncle Henry's suggestion was the one she followed. She had another reason which I learned many years later.

They moved to Atchison just after my father's graduation from law school. He was too young to practice law. Although he had passed the bar examination, he wouldn't turn twenty-one until the next October.

Maybe it was that summer that he began to play. He had never had the chance to be young before. He was ten the summer his father died. From then on he was the man of the house. He sat at his father's place at the head of the table and carved the meat. My mother said that he even went downtown in Carrollton and chose his mother's and sister's clothes. They didn't like to go out. Mother used to say, when I balked at changing out of my play clothes to come and greet her tea-time guests, that Dud had been shy when she was a girl. And my grandmother hadn't made her come and say hello to callers so she hadn't learned how to be gracious, and that was why she had grown up to be so odd, never marrying, never having a job or friends.

Perhaps it was while he was waiting to practice law that my father became a baseball player. He was actually good enough to be a professional, playing on one of the "farm" teams that trained players for the big time. He had played tennis during his college years, and now he excelled at that sport. In our dining room we had a row of silver cups that he had won.

My father's great hero was Teddy Roosevelt, the Rough Rider. On the wall by our staircase there was a drawing commemorating his death. Roosevelt was depicted astride a rearing horse, and he was waving his hat and grinning as he headed into the sunset. The title was "The Last Ride." Sometimes as I listened to my father talk I got Teddy Roosevelt mixed up with my Danish grandfather. I wondered if my father did too. I suspect that he used Teddy as an ideal. My father had been a sickly small boy, and my grandmother had kept him out of school until he was nearly eight. Perhaps she was overly concerned about him, or perhaps he really wasn't strong. Years later, after his death, when I met his cousin, she said that my father "was never allowed to" take part in sports. Because he was young for most of his classes, having passed through all of elementary and secondary school in just eight years, he probably was no match for many of the bigger, older boys. But by the time he came to Atchison, he was copying Teddy Roosevelt, who had turned himself from a weak child into a vigorous, strong man. My father tackled whatever sports were available, and years after his death I was told that he had been "a great athlete."

It was basketball that brought my parents together. Always at home with young people, perhaps eager to be someone's hero himself, my father became the coach for the Atchison High School basketball team. My uncle, Graham Henley, was on that team and invited the coach home to dinner. And there, playing gracious daughter of the family, was my mother. She had graduated from Miss Bennett's Boarding School in New York State, where she rode horseback (side saddle) on neighboring estates and went to chaperoned matinees in New York City. She visited cousins in Pennsylvania and had friends, including an admirer, in Toledo, Ohio.

Mother was part of a crowd of young people who came from the best families in Atchison. My father joined that group. He took part in the amateur theatricals which they performed. He often played the leading roles, while Mother had a smaller part. He told me that he had never had a date in college and managed to make the fact sound somehow admirable. I suspect, though, that the combination of his youth and social inexperience held him back.

In Atchison things were different. He started off fresh. He was a new and attractive man in a small town ready to find excitement in a newcomer. He was often asked for dinner at my grandparents' house. And one night, when my parents were both twenty-two and Mother had baked a cherry pie for dessert, he proposed. He always refused to eat cherry pie after that. He said he'd never really liked cherry pie, and he hadn't meant to propose that night, so it must have been the cherry pie that made him do it. Mother claimed that he proposed because she was going to Toledo the next day, and he was afraid she would become too enamored of his rival. After he left, Mother floated up the stairs to find Grandmother at the top, wrathful that Frederick had been allowed to stay so late. Mother defended herself with, "I'm engaged."

The engagement lasted for five years. Part of the reason for delaying the marriage was that young lawyers in Atchison didn't make much money. Even after my father went into Mr. Bailey's law office, he didn't earn much. But the biggest reason, Mother indicated, was that Dud and my other grandmother opposed the wedding. Mother said that my other grandmother took to her bed for a year so that my father wouldn't leave. I never knew the nature of her illness; Mother only sniffed when I asked her.

I don't know if Mother was ever a guest in that house on Fourth Street, or whether my other grandmother made the obligatory social call on my grandparents Henley after the engagement was announced. I have the impression that she and Dud refused to recognize it at all.

The long courtship must have become a way of life. My father was allowed to call every other evening. Grandmother, my mother told me (after I had reached the age when I encouraged the same caller too often), was "very wise." She realized that "propinquity" (a favorite word of my mother's, said with a knowing look, as if it meant something obscene) put a strain on young people in love, so she didn't permit my parents to see each other too often. My mother lived by her mother's rules until her twenty-eighth year.

And so my father would appear, usually with a box of candy from Gilbert's on Commercial Street under his arm. My mother told me that she would have preferred that he bring less candy and save his money to get her a bigger diamond. Years later, when she inherited Great-grandmother Graham's Tiffany-twist, double-diamond ring, she put it on her engagement finger with the wedding band and engagement ring. When I was small, she always said that you never wore anything on that finger except what your husband

Elizabeth, in garden

gave you, and then you never took that off. But my father didn't say anything about the addition. Great-grandmother's diamonds had a gold setting similar to Mother's, and the diamonds were the same cut, though larger. Together they looked like one large, handsome ring.

On summer evenings my parents sat on the porch swing while my father read or recited poetry—often his own—or sang love songs in "his funny voice" as my mother later described it. Sometimes they joined a group of young people at Gilbert's. It was an ice cream parlor then. It was only during my childhood that it became a tea room, with misty Maxfield Parrish-style murals and rose-shaded wall sconces and a back room that you could reserve for luncheons if you wanted a private party. It was at Gilbert's one evening that one of the young men made the remark which my father found so funny that he repeated it at appropriate times throughout his life. The menu listed, among its ice cream flavors, "Delmonico."

"Ah, Delmonico!" said the wit. "In other words, 'Vanilla!'"

It was one of those remarks that seems extremely funny to a group of high-spirited young persons already enjoying themselves. I have been conditioned to think of it still, whenever I hear the word "Delmonico." It has outlasted the man who made it. It has outlasted the mood of the moment and the laughter. And it brings back to me a sight I never saw: the ice cream-parlor chairs pushed around a table in the middle of Gilbert's front room, the overhead fan turning above it, and those young men and women, long gone now, all of them, laughing and joking and appreciating each other's sallies while Mr. and Mrs. Gilbert smile patiently at the soda fountain, waiting to take their orders.

In the summertime there were all-day excursions to Bean Lake for boating and picnics. After Aunt Flora and Uncle Chester married—young, the first in the crowd to do so—they could be chaperons. Then there were overnight stays at Bean Lake, the men in one cottage, the women (even, I think, Aunt Flora) in another. Sometimes they swam. My father, despite his other athletic skills, did not. He said that he was subject to cramps in the water. It was only in adulthood that I became aware of the desperate, silent battle he waged all of his life with claustrophobia. He never admitted that weakness, but gradually I recognized the significance of the doors which he always wanted open and his dislike of small, enclosed places. He accepted what he had to, fighting panic by himself. But I wondered if those moments of being unable to breathe in the water were his real reason for avoiding swimming.

During that long five years my parents began to keep a scrapbook of the activities which interested them both. The big purple suede book became crammed with their mementos, beginning with my father's first formal note asking "Miss Henley" to the Phi Gam dance at K.U. (why he, a nonfraternity man from Missouri U., was attending I never knew) and Mother's careful response to "Mr. Paulsen." On the next pages, there were dance programs, increasingly filled with my father's initials, and crumbling flowers, remnents of bouquets which he sent to my mother.

Other mementos proclaimed an Atchison social life both rich and varied. The Atchison Horse Show ran for three days in August of 1911. The program for August 29 had an illustrated cover and gold cord lacing. It listed eleven events, such as "Best Gentleman Rider, Local, (1st prize $5.00, 2nd prize $3.00, 3rd prize $2.00)" and "Best Girl Rider under 12 years, Local, (1st prize $3.00, 2nd prize $2.00)" with two entrants, total. Riders were named with their mounts ("Ned," "Dan," "Flash"). Donors, their gifts ranging from one dollar to two hundred dollars, were meticulously listed, including "H.H. Henley & Co., $5.00." There were programs from concerts, recitals put on by a school "of piano and musical theory," theater playbills and movie programs just as formally presented ("The House Next Door in Five Reels").

The Congregational Church sponsored a series of "sermons" by laymen on successive Sunday afternoons at four-thirty. Local business and professional men spoke, and on May 11, 1913, my father's topic was "The Administration of Law According to the Law of Christ." On the Sunday before, the Lieutenant Governor of Kansas, the man who would father my future playmates, Mary and Martha, spoke on "The Christianization of Law and Government."

Mother's prowess as "one of Atchison's most successful gardeners" was mentioned in the paper, where she was credited with making the family yard "one of the prettiest in town," having "cosmos in bloom and her dahlias have been blooming for two weeks," and, in 1916, for having "a receipt for Macaroni Pudding" accepted by *Good Housekeeping Magazine*. "Many guests" at a party given by Grandmother "complimented the daughter of the house on her womanly attainments."

Out-of-town guests were the occasion of much activity, fully reported in the society columns. Grandmother and Mother were noted as giving a tea and "Kensington" for a guest from Sheridan, Wyoming. She was Aunt Nannie, Grandmother's girlhood friend who had married and gone west to live. To Grandmother's amazement, Nannie had lived for a while in a sod house and had dealt with Indians. Atchison was much more civilized than that. The house at 1021 North Third Street had always had water piped into it. At first it came through the kitchen pump, vestigial in my childhood but still fun to try to work before Grandfather had the backyard well filled in. In Grandmother's photo album was a picture of cliff dwellings with Aunt Nannie's Christmas message "to the Ladies of the Reading Club."

The Reading Club was active in Mother's youth, though my

father took it less than seriously. A scrapbook photograph of Mother and some young lady friends bore my father's inscription: "Meeting of the Reading club. (Honest to goodness—look at the book.)"

Further social notes recorded the founding by "12 society people" of a new "dinner bridge club" to meet every other Tuesday night. Three married couples and six single persons (including my parents) made up the original select group. From then on, meetings (dinner, followed by bridge) were newspaper items. (A prim disclaimer appeared in the first announcement: "The club does not play for prizes.") Red-and-white was the color scheme at one meeting: "In the numerous courses of the dinner, red was carried out in the tempting viands."

Mother's turn as hostess came in time for an April Fool's dinner at which she served ice cream first, followed by finger bowls and then the numerous courses, ending with soup. Place cards in my father's hand, names spelled backwards, were pasted in the scrapbook with the newspaper account.

The reviews for the amateur theatricals in which my parents took part (with especially complimentary notices for my father), the pertinent programs and snapshots, filled pages. One series of photographs (taken outdoors to catch the light) showed restaged scenes from *Pollyanna*, in which my father was carrying a small girl who seemed to be asleep. He told me about that. He had promised the little girl, "If you stay absolutely still while we're on stage, I'll buy you a box of candy from Gilbert's."

When he kept his bargain with the candy, the child's mother said, "I warned her, 'Now, Mr. Paulsen's a busy man. He might forget the candy.' And she said, 'Well, if he does, I'll never actress for him again!'"

Out-of-town activities called, too. There were football programs from Lawrence, Kansas, and evidence of my father's own athletic activities. One clipping mentioned him as competing in the Missouri Valley championship tennis tournament under the auspices of the Kansas City Athletic Club, and another listed him as a winner in the Tri-State Tennis Tournament of 1913 (though the three states were not named). There was an account of a volleyball game with St. Joe and of a bowling tournament in which he starred. He evidently merited the comment which, years later at my mother's funeral, the funeral director made to me: "He was a great athlete."

Some cultural events in other cities were available. Mary Garden sang in *Thais* in St. Joe, the Ballet Russe was in Kansas City on March 14, 1916, and Arthur Nikisch was in Convention Hall in Kansas City with the London Symphony Orchestra on Wednesday evening, April 17, 1912. My parents had ample opportunity to indulge their mutual love of theater and concerts, a love which each retained. During the last year of his life, when his energy mysteriously flagged, the one event which my father wished to attend regularly was the St. Louis Symphony. It rested him, he said.

The activity that most energized my father during those waiting years—waiting to establish himself, waiting for marriage, waiting to create his own life—was political oratory. His violent affection for Teddy Roosevelt led him into the Bull Moose party, and he was official speaker at political rallies in neighboring states. An article from an unidentified paper complete with picture, stated that he "has accepted an appointment as one of the campaign speakers for the Progressive Party . . . (the) appointment came direct from the National Committee . . . William Allen White and Henry Allen recommended (him)."

Handbills listing him as "the Honorable" testified to his speaking at the "Court House, Beaver City," at Band Hall in Indianola, Nebraska, and there was a "special invitation to Ladies" to "Come Hear this Speech" in the "Afternoon at the Opera House" in Skidmore, Missouri. Mother, in a tiny show of independence, gave one dollar to the Taft campaign. The Roosevelt cause was lost, and by 1916 my father was a Republican speaker for Charles Evans Hughes. The handbill for his speech in Leona, Kansas, promised "Republican Speaker" with his name in big letters and, as a further inducement, "Good Music."

My parents must have read with mixed pleasure and pain the printed hints of their growing attachment. Repeated arch comments about their impending engagement preceded the formal announcement by years:

> An Atchison girl has been having her table and bed linen embroidered for approaching marriage, but the engagement has not yet been announced. She will marry a town man. She lives in North Atchison, and is an only daughter, but not an only child, she has one brother.
>
> A north Atchison couple, who have been attending fall weddings, are making mental notes of all the detailed arrangements down to the very tiniest bow of bridal tulle. And as we have said, "There's a reason."

The engagement wore on. Mother volunteered to teach kindergarten for a while and filled the hope chest made for her by my father. When the nefarious "propinquity" became too much of a problem, my grandparents sent her east to visit her cousins in Pennsylvania.

Grandmother, brushing my hair in our guest room in St. Louis during one of her visits, told me that "the family" had helped my father to get started. She said he didn't always tend to business as he should. Sometimes people would call his law office, and he wouldn't be there—he would just be out wandering around the town because nobody ever called. By the time she told me that, my father was a corporation lawyer, traveling all over the country.

I couldn't quite believe what Grandmother was telling me, but she seemed still to be cross about it. And Mother said that the only reason my father was elected City Attorney for Atchison was because of her. She said she went around to all of the old ladies who were friends of her grandmother Graham and said, "Please vote for Frederick. Then we can get married," and *they* said, "We don't know your young man, Elizabeth, but if *you* say he's all right, we'll vote for him."

So they did. My father won the election, and then he had enough money to get married. My other grandmother and Dud presented my father with a bill for debts they claimed against him, knowing, according to my mother, that he couldn't afford to pay them and get married too. But that ruse didn't work. My parents married just as World War I was beginning. He didn't pay his mother and sister anything. He said he didn't owe anything. But he gave his mother a note and paid it off in small amounts. The evidence was kept by my mother in her safe deposit box, which I examined after her death, forty-five years later.

Dud and my other grandmother didn't come to the wedding, although Mother said she sent them an invitation.

The wedding took place on the second of May in the Presbyterian Church. Lavender was my mother's favorite color, and friends had stripped their gardens of lilacs, which were tied to every pew. Mother's train was lined with wisteria satin.

Ever one to be prepared for possible eventualities, my father put his experience in theatricals to work. He buttered Mother's wedding ring to be sure he could get it on her finger on the first try. He also said he was perfectly capable of memorizing his lines and didn't need some nincompoop preacher feeding them to him, as if he were an idiot child. The minister said reassuringly, "I'll be right here, in case you forget," but my father glowered and said he wouldn't forget. Of course, he didn't. He had *said* he wouldn't

and he always kept his word. "Don't promise unless you can de-
liver," he used to tell me. "But once you say you'll do a thing, that's
a promise, whether you call it one or not. And you must always
keep a promise."

I don't know where they went on their honeymoon. Mother
said she called Grandmother from Kansas City because she thought
Grandmother might be feeling lonely. And Mother woke up crying
one night when they were away. "What's the matter?" my father
asked, and Mother sniffled, "It's *dark!*"

"Of course it's dark. It's night," my father said. He told that
story many times over the years, to prove, perhaps, how logic could
be applied to the silliest situations. My mother said that she was
used to the sounds and lights of street cars going near my grandparents' house, and she didn't know where she was for a moment.
Anyway, she said, she was getting sick. She developed what she
called "quinsey," a severe sore throat, and had to go back home
and let Grandmother nurse her to health before she and my father
could move into their rented bungalow on Second Street.

I don't know whether the wedding date had been at all influenced
by this country's entry into World War I the month before. Probably not. Wedding plans in that day, that town, took time and were
accomplished in a leisurely, traditional fashion. And their generation knew little, then, about wars.

My father always announced that one didn't wait to be called
when one's country needed one. One went out and enlisted. He
enlisted and was proud to say so. But it took him a year to get
into the branch of service that he wanted. Finally my mother closed
up the little bungalow and went back to Grandmother's house
while my father reported for duty to train as a naval aviator in
Pensacola.

Aviation was a new and hazardous military activity. The planes
were flimsy, without sophisticated instruments, and many a young

trainee flew out across the bay only to lose his way out of sight of land when his compass failed. The first time my father soloed, his instructor asked, "Can you fly around a storm?"

With his eternal show of confidence, my father, who had read about the procedure in books, said he could.

"Good," said the instructor. "There's a storm coming up. Go fly around it." My father did.

Just to be a part of aviation branded one a hero. There was a specialness and a camaraderie so great that graduating classes had a yearbook, as college classmates did. There were so few naval aviators that their distinctive uniform, a green color different from any used by either the Army or the regular Navy, was often unidentified even by other branches of the military. The ensign's star on the shoulder was sometimes mistaken for the mark of a one-star general of some allied army, and my father enjoyed saying, "At ease, Colonel," when a high ranking United States officer would hop to with a snappy salute.

All of these factors—the daring, the feeling of being part of a very select fraternity, the nobility of it all—appealed to my father and let him live the role he had chosen for himself. His one stated disappointment was that his only assignment subsequent to gaining his commission was as an instructor in navigation at M.I.T. in Boston. My mother joined him there. He was, he said, to lead a squadron of planes in the spring drive, but the war ended before then. Though he professed regret, I eventually realized that, had he had that assignment, I might never have come to be.

So their war ended. My uncle Graham, who as an artillery officer had survived every major battle in which the American troops took part, came home by way of Boston and caught the often lethal flu. Mother, wearing a surgical mask, visited him in the hospital. Daily she heard the dirge as the death march was played at the funerals of those who didn't survive. Uncle Graham did.

They all went back to Grandmother's house. My parents moved

Frederick Paulsen, World War I

into the house on Fifth Street, owned by my grandfather. Reestablishing his law practice, my father earned practically nothing the first month. Uncle Graham settled down at home and went to work in the flour mill, of which Grandmother's brother was president. Grandfather sent off to Tiffany's in New York for a diamond dinner ring for Grandmother, because she had been so brave while Uncle Graham was overseas.

And finally, my parents got around to having me.

The taste of politics which had begun with the old ladies of Atchison cooperating to make him City Attorney had intrigued my father, and he became active within the Republican party. Eventually, he was appointed Assistant Attorney General for the state of Kansas. During my babyhood he worked during the week in the capitol at Topeka. One of his jobs involved investigating corruption in the highway department, and he had a major part in uncovering a scandal. Evidently some powerful and dangerous persons were involved. Anonymous word came to my father that he had better not show himself on the streets of Topeka after dark. His reaction was showy and automatic. Each evening after dinner, he slowly walked the main streets, up one, down another, pausing to linger by lighted shop windows, being sure he was visible. He was not attacked.

As he told the story, I imagined him fearless. My father wasn't afraid of anything. But perhaps he was and met the challenge anyway, knowing that if he didn't, he would have shown that he could be intimidated. Maybe he was simply obstinate and didn't want anyone telling him what to do. Maybe his flair for the dramatic took over, and he enjoyed playing the hero's role. His times and his personality demanded that role, and he played it impressively. Two generations later, a grandson born after his death had occasion to walk a lonely road at night. There had been threats for him, too, but remembering the story of his grandfather, borrowing that courage for a companion, he walked at his usual pace, knowing that if he ran, he would have to run out of town and never come back. The dramatic gesture once more was a protection; the threatened attack did not occur. Dead then for nearly thirty years, my father was again counted as a hero.

Another of his assignments involved representing the state of Kansas against the Telephone Company. Scouted by some of the legal staff of the corporation, my father was offered a position with the legal department of the southwestern branch, headquartered in St. Louis.

My uncle told me later that my father had wondered if it was ethical to take a job with the other side and talked to my grandfather about it. Grandfather had recognized the opportunity and urged that he take it. So the devotee of Teddy Roosevelt, the trust buster, became an employee for a monopolistic corporation which he embraced with all of the one-sided fervor of his nature.

My parents packed their possessions and moved to St. Louis. The days of Atchison as home were over. From then on, Atchison was where Grandmother's house was.

4

Moving

It didn't occur to me until much later—really not until after her death—how difficult the move from Atchison was for Mother. Of course, being only a year-and-a-half old then, I don't remember the move. Except for one thing—and I swear I remember it.

Mother and Lena, the blond farm girl who moved with us from Atchison, and I had come to St. Louis on the sleeper. My father had preceded us. I don't remember the trip or the reunion, but I do recall the next event. My father, ever one to make an occasion special, took us to breakfast on the Statler Hotel roof. I don't recall getting there, but the sudden vignette is clear in my mind, forever real, remembered by no one else.

We four are seated at a table. Across the roof, in my line of vision, two high walls come together at right angles and in the corner, atop the ledge, is a large pot of trailing vines. We are open to the sky. I am in a high chair in the center of things, or so it seems to me. My father is on the side of the table to my left. Mother and Lena are distributed on the other sides. During the last days in Atchison, during my father's absence, I have learned to say "egg." I am waiting for my big moment.

My father, holding a menu, is taking everyone's order. Finally he turns to me. "And what will you have?" he says with the grown-up deference which he shows toward any guest, even a child.

I am drawn back, ready. "*Egg!*" I shout on cue.

My father drops his menu, falls back in his chair, is overcome. I shriek with glee, while Mother and Lena applaud.

A curtain drops on my memory.

I remember nothing of our arrival at our new home. But even now I could draw a plan of that house. It was a rented house. I suppose that, at the time, my parents couldn't afford to buy a house, but more than that they probably weren't sure that the move—and the job—would be permanent.

They chose a suburb on the Missouri Pacific train route out from St. Louis, a more comforting similarity to a self-contained small town than a city location could have afforded. The house was owned by a large white-haired German, a Mr. Bauer, who lived across the street. Now, two generations later, Mr. Bauer's descendants own business property all over the area, and none would call himself German.

Next door to us, on the corner, lived Judge Ott. He was enormous! But Mrs. Ott was skinny, and their grown-up daughter Elizabeth wasn't anything noticeable. Judge Ott had a model A Ford which had one front seat. With difficulty, Judge and Mrs. Ott could sit side by side, though Judge Ott took up most of the space. When the whole family went out together all dressed up, Elizabeth had to sit on Mrs. Ott's lap.

Next door on the other side lived the Flahertys. They were the opposite of the Otts. Mr. Flaherty was skinny, and Mrs. Flaherty was fat. They had lots of children, more than my mother approved of. My parents thought the Flahertys foolish and irresponsible, especially Tom, Mr. Flaherty. Billy, who was my age, told me proudly how his father tried to beat the trains at the crossing, and how one time he was on the track as the gate came down, and the metal support pierced the canvas top of their touring car. My father said that was typical of Tom Flaherty.

Sometimes I was included in Mr. Flaherty's fecklessness. What could I do? He was a grown-up and set the pace. Once Thomas, the eldest boy (later to become a priest), was hit on his ankle by a golf ball. His foot was dramatically encased in plaster, enhancing the feeling of secret awe I already had for him. Mr. Flaherty took all of us children, all the Flahertys and me, in the touring car to the doctor to have Thomas's cast changed. And he *carried* Thomas, a big boy, from the car as we shrieked in delight, and Thomas, the quiet one, looked abashed. On the way home, Mr. Flaherty bought us all ice cream cones—*in the morning*! I was never supposed to eat between meals. But Mr. Flaherty was in charge, so with a delicious sense of guilt I acceded.

The Flahertys led me astray in other ways. Once Billy and I sat on our tricycles, the fence between our yards dividing us, while Mother and Mrs. Flaherty scraped at the cow manure on our feet and the wheels and pedals of our trikes. We had been totally un-aware of picking up any such detritus on our trek through the meadow at the far end of the street. Mrs. Flaherty seemed rather amused. Mother was trying not to be sick.

And there was the sugar bread. The Flahertys were given a snack of white bread spread with butter and sugar and then held under the sink faucet for a good soaking. I determined to accept the treat, but as the hired girl held the slice on her open palm and prepared to turn on the tap, I said, "No water on mine, please."

She froze. "You don't want water on yours?"

"No."

She seemed to find that strange. But she gave me the slice of bread, and I took it across the street where I hid behind a telephone pole to eat it. Again, it was a morning.

Mother felt that she was surrounded by persons who were not her "kind." Even when she first examined the house we were to rent, she came away with distaste. The past occupants were not good housekeepers. The drip pan under their ice box was overflowing.

There was one woman living a few blocks away whom Mother considered a lady. That was Mrs. Woodbridge. She was older than Mother and had three sons, all grown or nearly so. They were Jim, Hugh, and Frank. Frank sometimes accompanied his parents when they came to play bridge with my father and mother. I would be in my nightie, ready for bed. Frank would play with me in the living room until I was taken upstairs for the night. When Frank married Gretchen, I was allowed to go to the wedding, and even after we moved there were some Sunday excursions with Mr. and Mrs. Woodbridge, Frank and Gretchen, and their little girl.

There were a few Atchison people in the St. Louis area, but they were scattered and not easily available. Mother's friend Aunt Gertrude and her husband, Uncle Will, and their son, George R. (R. for Robertson, the name of the town in South Africa from which Uncle Will had come), lived in a flat in the city. Aunt Gertrude's parents were also in the city, and my grandfather and Aunt Gertrude's father had been best man at each other's weddings. And there was Mrs. Crane, married to a doctor and living with their three children in the West End of the city. Though Mother and Mrs. Crane were about the same age, they hadn't been close friends in Atchison. Mother had gone to the private preparatory school, and Mrs. Crane had gone to "the public." Now, though, Mrs. Crane's children went to private schools, and I eventually attended the public suburban ones.

Anyway, it wasn't easy for Mother to visit these scattered friends. It was years before we bought our Jewett touring car with the isinglass curtains that had to be hastily snapped in when a rain storm came up. So any jaunts took place by streetcar.

I always got sick. The stale smell of old tobacco smoke and human sweat which permeated the wicker seats of the unaired cars overcame me every time, and I would arrive at Mrs. Crane's or Aunt Gertrude's with my pale blue crepe de chine coat stained and reeking. So visits, though doggedly undertaken by my lonely mother, were not the easy outings they had been in Atchison.

But most of all, no one knew who she really was. The names Graham and Henley meant nothing in St. Louis, nor did references to "the family mill." Though my father was eventually to gain a fine professional reputation, that hadn't happened yet. I suppose that my parents had parties in that first rented house, but I don't remember any. Perhaps they didn't know enough people to make up a suitable guest list.

Just before I was six, we moved again. My parents had chosen their mecca, the suburb next to the one in which we first lived. They had selected the school which I was to attend and had bought a lot. Plans for a house, a Dutch colonial, were drawn up. But one Sunday when we were exploring the area, my parents found Their House. It was a newly-remodeled early Victorian to which closets and bathrooms had been added to provide the necessities of the '20s. It stood on a lot-and-a-half—more ground than the surrounding houses had—in a one-block street carved out of the original estate.

Cupping his hands against the blank windows, my father peered into his dream library. All one wall was open shelves, and the west wall, opposite the fireplace, was lined with lead-paned, glass-enclosed cases. My father said that fine books should always be kept behind glass. He was starting to collect first editions.

The house was bigger than that of my grandparents. Downstairs were halls, front and back, a music room where Great-grandmother Graham's piano could be ensconced, a living room, the library with a windowed alcove in which my father's chair was later placed, the dining room with a bay and built-in cabinets with long drawers for tablecloths, the big butler's pantry with its copper-lined sink

Elizabeth, on porch of St. Louis home

and the counter where my cod liver oil bottle was kept, the kitchen, and a separate room called "the breakfast room," another bow to the mode of the '20s. It was never so used, and Mother eventually lined it with cabinets for canned goods and finally, after Repeal, my father's liquor supply. A porch with pillars and a porte cochere went across the front of the house (the former owner had been southern and wanted her white columns) and a screened porch was off the kitchen.

It was a large house for a family of three. By that time, my parents knew that there would be no more children. But I felt no surprise at moving into so large a house. To me it was simply home.

All of the years of my growing up there, the doors were always open to my friends. A playmate could stay for dinner on the spur of the moment. Mother later said that they wanted to make up to me for being an only child. I never felt deprived. It was later that I felt the burden of having too much—too much of my parents' attention, too much the weight of their unfulfilled desires, of being too much their reason for staying together.

My parents gave parties, large dinners with my father's Telephone Company associates or bridge parties with tables throughout the downstairs rooms for the ladies of the Monday Club or the Wednesday Club. Mother didn't talk so much about the Henleys or the Grahams or the family mill, but introduced herself as "Mrs. Frederick Paulsen," with her address. The green Oakland in the garage was supplanted by a blue Oakland when the time came for a trade-in. The younger Crane girl and I became good friends, and she was our guest on northern vacations.

It was the prosperous '20s, when the sun was to continue to shine. By the time of the Depression, my father's position was secure enough that I was spared the worry that others must have known. So I lived in that house until I was twenty, when, rebelling for the first time against my startled parents, I announced my decision to marry before the coming war should overwhelm us.

My father made my choice a rejection of him. There was nothing I could do to pacify him unless I gave up my own wishes—and that I would not. I wondered, during that strained summer, whether he realized that he was behaving toward me much as his mother had toward him so many years ago. For by then, I knew the story.

5

Bedrooms

Sometimes when I was very small, as a special treat I slept with Grandmother in the Pink Bedroom. It opened into Grandfather's room and had been so designed for my mother as a baby to whom Grandmother wanted easy access at night.

After Grandmother had brushed my hair the "wrong way" to make it curl, I would lie in the cool linen sheets smelling of lavender and watch Grandmother take down her white hair. In the daytime she piled it on her head and held it there with a transparent hair net and dozens of silvery hair pins, some bone and many more wiggly wire ones. Miraculously, the hair fell, shining and wavy, down her back. As she brushed the nightly hundred strokes, she would show me where there were still strands of brown and the yellow it had once been. I thought it marvelous that my grandmother had hair of three colors. No one hinted that hers was an accomplishment I might one day duplicate. Grandmother was dissatisfied that now all of her hair appeared white.

Drowsily waiting for Grandmother to come to bed, I would look around the familiar room. From my unaccustomed position in the four-poster, the room seemed intriguingly new, but it became comfortingly familiar as I picked out each landmark. . . .

The desk at which Grandmother wrote her weekly letters to us sat at right angles to the window with the bird feeder. The desk had been a Christmas present to my mother when she attained "big girl" status. It was given at a family Christmas at Great-grandmother Graham's house. A younger cousin, Eloise, received a dollhouse which my mother coveted but was thought to be too old for. The desk was a poor second.

In the window bay on the front wall were two chairs and over each a picture taken at the time of my parents' engagement. One was of my long-jawed father, the other of my mother in profile, looking dreamily into the distance, a bemused half-smile on her lips.

Over the fireplace were two oval framed pictures of my grand-parents near the time of their marriage. My grandfather's fierce handlebar mustache did not change the impression of vulnerability made by his high exposed forehead and the sensitive expression he shared with my mother. Years later the pictures went to the attic. When, as an adult, I asked for them, a maid said that my aunt Mavis once wrapped them up and went down the back stairs with them under her arm. She said she wanted to put mirrors in the gold frames; no one ever wanted those old pictures anyway. When I let it be known that I did and wondered aloud at a family dinner whatever happened to them, the pictures, without frames, reappeared in the attic, rather better dusted than when they had left. . . .

Then just as my eyes were closing, Grandmother in her thin embroidered batiste gown that smelled of the garden tuberoses, dried and tucked in her bureau drawers, Grandmother, still the mistress of her house, would slip into bed beside me and turn off the rose-shaded light.

Most nights, though, I slept in the Blue Bedroom, the room of my mother's girlhood. Seven-sided, it was built over the front porch. It stood at the head of the stairs, and my uncle Graham, coming home from a date, used to stop in to talk to "Sis" about the evening. A full-length mirror was on the closet wall, a place for young girls to admire their ball gowns. And after a dance, back in this room the same young girls hushed their nervous laughter and hid behind the curtains, presenting only shadowy silhouettes to the young men serenading below:

> "Moon of the summer night . . .
> Watch! while in slumbers light
> She sleeps, my lady sleeps,
> Sheee—sleeps—
> She sleeps,
> My—y—y la—a—dy sleeps."

Windows at three angles still did not bring in much breeze on hot Kansas nights. The thin starched curtains barely stirred. I knew where the two declivities in the mattress were and how to curl around them in the big walnut bed with its carved headboard reaching almost to the ceiling.

I woke, my hair and nightgown damp, to the sound of cooing pigeons. They visited from the belfry of the Catholic church two blocks away, making their stately morning perambulations on the wide brick-paved street under the elms. Sedately they affirmed that all was as it should be.

On hot summer afternoons when I was asked to "rest," if not to nap, such a habit being demeaning to my age, I sometimes was allowed to have The Quilt. Made by my grandfather's Quaker mother, it was a vibrant mélange of scraps of everyone's best dress. Backed by purple changeable taffeta, edged with red satin painted with flowers, it was good for an hour's examination. Would I choose to have a dress of this sapphire velvet? Or of the pale pink satin, sprigged with tiny flowers? If you turned the quilt one way you could read Great-grandmother Henley's initials, E.S.H., near the middle. Another turn and in the corner was an embroidered date,

1884. A flag with thirteen stars was appliqued near one border, and—upside down if you had the flag in position—two inexplicable Chinamen with a parasol were embroidered on some dull black stuff.

Mostly I used the small dark wicker desk in my bedroom for drawing or for letter writing. But one fall I used it for school work. My mother and I came directly from the family summer vacation to stay in Atchison for several weeks. There was a sleeping sickness epidemic reported in St. Louis. My father urged that, for my safety, Mother and I visit my grandparents until the epidemic subsided. Mother, always anxious in matters of health, concurred. Later she decided—and much later told me—that it was not my father's concern for me but his desire to further an affair begun at the summer resort that caused the decision. A good lawyer, he argued his case convincingly.

So that fall I was tutored by a retired teacher of my mother's, Miss Florence, and "checked" in math by my grandfather. Grandfather was impatient with my work but tried not to show it. Testily pointing out my errors, he indicated his irritation at what I "hadn't had." Modern schools clearly didn't do their jobs. He had taught in a one-room school when he was a young man in Pennsylvania. He had built up the fire in the mornings and built up his students, too.

The spare bedroom with its brass bed and half-bath had been Uncle Graham's when he lived at home. I remember him shaving in his undershirt and trousers before the medicine cabinet mirror. I must have been about three. By the time I was three-and-a-half I had been flower girl in his wedding, and he and Aunt Mavis had moved to the Fifth Street house. As I watched him scraping his cheeks, careful to preserve his mustache, he turned and planted a daub of lather on my nose, laughing at me. I was offended. I couldn't have explained it then, but his laughing *at* me shattered the camaraderie of a moment before and separated us. It was the separation that I minded.

Mother and Grandmother comforted me by saying Graham was always a tease. Mother said he used to chase her up to Great-grandmother Graham's, brandishing his toy tomahawk. Great-grandmother would appear at my mother's shrieks saying, "Graham, I'll take my slipper to you!" Uncle Graham said afterwards that he really hadn't intended to cut off Mother's head; he just liked to see her long legs fly over the ground.

This room looked out towards Great-grandmother Graham's house and over the long stretch of garden between the two properties. Summer days I would hear the sash window flung up and Grandmother call, "*Oh*, Majors!" until the yardman came to stand humbly, looking up to receive Grandmother's instructions about what *not* to do to the petunias in the north bed.

Occasionally I was put to bed in the spare room. One such time was Christmas Eve during the years in which Grandmother still slept in the Pink Bedroom and my parents occupied the Blue Bedroom. With Grandfather and my parents mysteriously busy, I was tucked into the brass bed, and Grandmother was commissioned to read me a Christmas bedtime story. The room lay directly below the largest attic storeroom. As Grandmother read, I became aware of a bumping and scraping sound above us.

"Grandma! *Shh!*" She obediently stopped reading. "I think I hear Santa Claus's reindeer on the roof!" We listened, staring at each other. Grandmother admitted that the sound very likely *was* Santa Claus's sleigh. I'd better go to sleep right away, because he must be visiting our house early.

During my teens I awoke one morning in the Blue Bedroom feeling sick. I *was* sick. I was moved into the spare room to be near the facilities of the half-bath which I obviously needed. Eventually

Dr. Robbins, father of my childhood playmate Ann Bobbie, came to poke my stomach and take blood from my finger. A phone call confirmed his original suspicion: I had appendicitis. Mother and Aunt Mavis and I boarded the Missouri River Eagle and spent a restless night in a drawing room, I, in unaccustomed luxury in the lower berth, Aunt Mavis above me in the upper, and Mother across from me on the "shelf" from which she could spring into nocturnal action if needed. We were met at the station in the early morning by our family doctor with an ambulance.

"Please," I said as I was strapped onto the stretcher, "May I have the siren?" The amused driver complied, and we went through the deserted streets—and even through one red light—with the siren blaring. Later, I proudly learned that my appendix was "ready to burst" when removed.

It was into the spare room that Grandmother moved when Grandfather felt she needed constant attention. The walls were then papered with yellow flowers, for yellow was Grandmother's favorite color, forbidden to her as a little blond girl. ("Not yellow clothes and yellow hair," her mother decreed.) The brass bed gave way to a hospital bed. A nurse slept on a cot in the window alcove.

Yet Grandmother still presided. Here she summoned Marguerite and Rosemary, the two warring farm sisters who kept house and fought with each other. ("Now, girls, you should get along. You're *sisters*. I never had a sister.") Here she sat in a chair by the window when, at twenty, I made the trip to Atchison to tell her of my engagement. And here, on the wall between the windows, as close to her old home as possible, hung Great-grandmother Graham's picture. She looked more pleasant than I remembered her, but not much.

Once Grandfather and I were sitting with Grandmother in this cheery room, now the Yellow Bedroom. They were both in their eighties by then, and Grandmother spent much of her time resting. But she liked to have company. "Grandmother," I said, "how many men wanted to marry you?"

Grandfather stirred and looked alert. Grandmother gazed off into the distance, ignoring him. "Fi—noo—six," she corrected herself.

Grandfather snorted.

"There was this one fellow," mused Grandmother. "He came to call during the winter. And he was wearing a ring. On his way out he slipped on the ice, and the ring flew off of his hand. We searched and searched, but we couldn't find it. So then he wrote and said if we found it, I should keep it. That," said Grandmother, turning away from Grandfather to look at me, "would have meant we were engaged."

"Well, I never heard about *that*!" said Grandfather.

"When the snow melted in the spring, we found the ring. I sent it back," said Grandmother primly, still addressing me.

"Was he the same one who gave you the opera glasses?"

"No," said Grandmother dreamily. "That was someone else. Of course, I knew it wasn't proper to accept such an expensive gift from a man unless you were engaged to him. But he pointed out that he'd had my name engraved on them, so I *had* to keep them." By now the opera glasses were mine, a dainty set with mother-of-pearl tubes, Grandmother's (and my) name engraved across the gold nose piece. They were still in their original worn leather case with a tiny gold butterfly on the clasp.

"*He* wanted to marry you?"

"Yes. You see, he thought if he could just get me to keep the glasses, we'd be engaged. Then there was this *other* fellow . . . "

"Don't listen to her, Ellen!" Grandfather exploded. "She's senile. She's getting childish in her old age."

Grandmother went right on. "And *that* fellow . . . "

I realized with an inward chortle that my grandparents were flirting with each other.

Grandfather's room, the sunny Red Bedroom across the hall, had been theirs together when they were younger. Even after she moved into the Pink Bedroom, Grandmother still set the treadle sewing machine up in the bay and spread patterns out on Grandfather's round table. On those occasions, two or three times a year, when the seamstress came for several days of intensive sewing, Grandmother made sure that the noon meal was especially nice. The murmured explanation was that the specialness was for the benefit of the seamstress. But it may also have been compensation for Grandfather, whose room was taken over and who had to live with the accumulation of cloth snippets and bits of thread for several days.

Grandfather had some dumbbells in his closet, though by now he used them only for demonstrations for me. He used to exercise with them regularly, just as he used to play volleyball at the Y with my father and uncle. Once, I was told, my father had bitten Grandfather on the head. They both went after a ball, and Grandfather had come up under my father, and my father's teeth had hit my grandfather's head. My parents were courting at the time, and my father was a little embarrassed. But I kept thinking how it would be to bite my grandfather's bald head. Had my father come down on the hair part or the skin part? How had it tasted?

Above the bureau was a picture of my bearded great-grandfather Henley. There is the same high forehead of my grandfather and my mother, but a tougher look. Whatever Great-grandfather's sensitivities, three round-trips from Pennsylvania to California, starting with the Gold Rush, put a greater value on other qualities. Though bred a Quaker, he relied on something other than gentle persuasion during his days in the West. He joined the vigilantes in California and once broke a bottle of catsup over the head of a man who tried to rob the store he had set up to supply miners. Then he leapt over the counter, grabbed the catsup-smeared robber by the shirt front, and drubbed him down the street, while bystanders cried, "Mr. Henley, you're killing that man!"

And once while he was crossing the country, an Indian shot an arrow through his hat. Said my grandfather, "Father got down off the wagon and took the bow away from the Indian and brought it home to us boys." I had always envisioned my great-grandfather, bearded as in the picture, an arrow piercing his hat, silently holding out his hand as he stared down the dumbfounded Indian who meekly surrendered his bow. I was grown before I realized that the scene was never played, at least not like that.

The last bedroom, between the shared family bathroom and the back stairs, was the maid's. For one glorious summer it was a place of enchantment and shared secrets for me and the current—though soon to be departing—occupant. She was going to be a bride! In the afternoons, the door closed and shades drawn against the blazing western sun, we sat on her bed and marveled over the growing contents of her cedar chest and the hidden packages in the closet. Of all of that marvelous treasure for her home-to-be I remember only one item: a framed picture of a timber wolf standing on a rugged mountain. For some unfathomable reason I, who had never seen a wild animal outside of a zoo, had in school written a poem about just such a wolf. I recited it, and the bride found it wonderful—so wonderful, in fact, that she asked me to write it out so she could hang it in her new home, right next to the picture. Always eager for immortality, I obligingly copied out:

The Lone Wolf
The lone wolf stands on a ledge so high
The night is clear and bright.
There is a gleam in his sparkling eye
On this cold and frosty night.

It went on like that for several more stanzas, none of them getting any better. There was absolutely no character development on the part of the wolf. Nothing much happened to the night, either.

⁖   ⁖   ⁖

The house held us all together, those who had gone before and stayed alive for me through stories, those whose lives had been lived here, those of us who touched here only to move on. Each night in the darkness we lay in our rooms, doors open to the heavily moving air and to each other, linked by the living that had brought each to this place, this time, secure in our parts, sheltered by the house that defined us all.

Even when the heat caused sleeplessness, there were no night terrors. Grandfather mounted the stairs outside my door and gave the hall light switch three clicks, which turned out the lights both upstairs and down. The library clock struck the Westminster chimes on the quarter hour. The calm of the quiet house brought more rest than sleep could.

And on those summer mornings of childhood I awakened always to a sense of peace. The ordered household was running as it should. Grandmother was giving instructions in the kitchen, planning the food I liked as she arranged the flowers for the day. Grandfather had driven the Hudson to his office and would return at noon. Late breakfast was served whenever I awoke, bacon, last night's rolls, split, buttered, and toasted, and a glass of cool milk. The day was properly begun. Grandmother and the pigeons had seen to that.

6

Children of Summer

"*Bootsey!*" my mother said—and giggled. She wasn't sounding like a mother. She was sounding like a schoolgirl. She was sounding like *me*, when a boy showed off by being silly. The boy in question was Mr. Edmonds, father of my friend, Sally, with whom I had spent the afternoon. Now he stood, leaning his forearms on the window frame of Grandfather's Hudson, while Mother sat behind the wheel. Mr. Edmonds' face was decorated with the lipstick that Sally and I had painted on it, and his sparse forelock was tied with a blue bow. Deadpan, he had come out to greet Elizabeth, friend of his youth. She had been that person before she was my mother.

But didn't she realize that now she was *completely* my mother? And why did she keep on giggling that way, calling into being a girlhood that should have been past? Sometimes within the safe cocoon of the Atchison of my childhood, brief flashes of what had once been would shatter, for only a moment, my view of what seemed knowable and permanent. This otherness had taken place without me and somehow excluded me. Mostly there were only small things, quickly over, but they signified other lives, other claims than mine.

There was the birthday party at Uncle Henry's house, a big, square white stucco building set high on a terrace several blocks from Grandmother's house. Uncle Henry, also big and square with white hair, looked in on the party briefly and then departed, leaving the stage to his wife, Aunt Nellie.

I had a special right to be there, not just because I was close in age to the two boys, Peter and Harold. My father called their father "Uncle Henry," and I did too. My father didn't call Mother's uncle "Uncle Wesley," but "Mr. Graham." In the way I didn't quite understand then, Uncle Henry was related to my father—and therefore to me. He was, in fact, the only relative of his own with whom my father was ever in touch in Atchison. Or so I thought.

But at the party, here was *my* grandmother sitting on the couch surrounded by a group of children, reading to them all. I snuggled up as close as possible, proud that she was the star of the moment but eager to remind everyone—including her—that she was mine.

Grandmother was reading a story that told you how to eat soup in the proper way. Gravely, she demonstrated: you moved the spoon away from you, *this* way, not toward you, *that* way. She was impartially approving as the children mimicked her gesture. But I already knew how to eat soup. Surely Grandmother should acknowledge that?

What must Uncle Henry's brief glance at us all have meant to him? As I later learned, he had already lost to death two wives and three children. A children's party, presided over by a happy wife a generation his junior with his two handsome young sons in attendance, must have seemed at last a bright spot after the shadows. He must have gone off relieved and content.

But his respite was to be brief. Within only a few years, Aunt Nellie was to die of cancer. And one day several years after that, Uncle Henry and Peter returned to see ten-year-old Harold in the driveway. Harold gave them one look and ran into the house and upstairs. There was an explosion. By the time they reached him, Harold lay dead of a shotgun blast in the upstairs bathroom.

An accident? Was he handling a forbidden gun? Atchison people said he missed his mother.

But none of that cast shadows yet. For now, we snuggled together on the couch, laying claims to Grandmother's attention. I knew I would win, and Peter and Harold didn't really care. It was their party.

Then there was the matter of the blue crayon. I was spending the day with my friends, Mary and Martha, the last two of a large brood of children. Their grandfather had been a United States Senator, and Atchison people still spoke of him proudly, though he was long dead, so long that Mary and Martha had never known him. His fame lent glamour to his family for succeeding generations. When one of his several sons married the woman who would be Mary and Martha's mother, my mother, then a little girl playing with dolls, idolized the new bride. She named one of her dolls for her, though with a respectful "Mrs." before her name. And she was given a small silver-backed hat brush with the Senator's name engraved on it. The gift was a mark of fondness between the families.

By the time I knew Mary and Martha, their mother was no longer called "Mrs." by my mother. They had entered the same generation and called each other by their first names. There were ten or twelve children in the family, so many that I never met them all, but I took pride in being able to recite their names in sequence. The first, I knew, was Ruth Constance, a mythical creature grown up and living in Paris. Double names were soon given up in that family; there was a need for so many. All of the children were vigorous and healthy-seeming, though one son had died of pneumonia. I heard that his mother had sat by his bedside all night and pumped a machine to help him breathe.

But this summer afternoon was unclouded by such memories or forebodings. Mary and Martha and I were spread out on the hall floor of their big white frame house, sharing crayons in some coloring project. Philip, old enough so that he was seldom part of our activities, was for some reason—perhaps boredom—with us. I wanted the blue crayon, and Mary did too. Philip told me with some animus that Mary should have it. I had a clear demonstration of family solidarity. Mary was Philip's *sister*, and I was the outsider, without rights. But Mary was not one to carry on a feud, especially since she got the blue crayon.

Once Mary took me to school with her. I had never been to school, being then probably four to Mary's more adult five. Martha, a year younger than I, was not included in the invitation. I was being shown what school was like, as I would be going next year at home. We all sat at desks, though it must have been kindergarten. Mother had been a substitute teacher in that school. She told how some of the little children missed the naps they had been used to, and when she had them put their heads on their desks to rest in the warm afternoon, some of them fell asleep. But one child was wiggly and restless, and Mother would take him on her lap and hold his hands while she read aloud so he wouldn't bother the other children.

But I neither wiggled nor fell asleep. I wanted to do whatever seemed proper without calling undue attention to myself. Some attention came my way, but I recall only welcoming smiles and Mary's evident pride in being able to show off something new— me. The teacher was kind. She wore a sort of floaty dark blue dress which left her arms bare. On one arm she had a spongy raised mole. My father had one of those, on the back of one knee. Her mole, her smile, her floaty dress all impressed me. But I was most impressed by the cookies with pink-and-white icing which she gave us. School must be very nice.

∴ ∴ ∴

Next door to Grandmother's house but down the hill was a little frame house. It seemed especially small, one story next to Grandmother's three stories, set high on a terrace. The families in that house changed frequently, but there was often a little girl there. Before one of my visits, Grandmother, tending the flowers, would have made her acquaintance over the fence, and I would have a ready-made playmate. From the bathroom window I could look down on the kitchen door of the little house. Shrouded in a sun-fresh Turkish towel after my afternoon bath in the clawfooted tub, I could shout to my emerging friend to *wait*! I would be right out.

Across the street from Grandmother's house was Forrest's Greenhouse. The garages and greenhouses were on one side, the family's white house next to them, and the growing fields of flowers were on the other side. As Grandmother was something of a gardener herself, famous for her flowers, in fact, she seldom bought from Mr. Forrest. Anyway, she wasn't overly fond of his sisters, Miss Rose and Miss Violet, who presided over the house. Grandmother had grown up with the Forrests living on the same street. When Grandmother was a child and Great-grandmother made her a dress, Miss Rose's mother made her one just like it. If Great-grandmother added a sash or something to change it a little, Miss Rose's mother added one, too. That just showed how small they had always been.

Not that Miss Rose and Miss Violet were physically small. They were fat and talkative. Their brother, Melvin, who ran the greenhouse, was a tall, taciturn man, a little scary because he was so silent. He seemed to be forever rounding the corner of his house on the way to the greenhouse, his arms straining with the weight of two heavy buckets. Melvin, Jr., tall, thin, and as silent as his father, made similar journeys. But it was with Alice and Bertram Forrest that I played. Alice, tall and thin like her father and brother, gentle and patient with a younger girl, was someone I liked and—somehow—pitied a little. Alice, with her soft smile, sewing on kewpie doll dresses with me, though perhaps she was a little old for that, seemed glad of my company. She and Bertram, a year younger than I, could cross the street to Grandmother's house to play with me, but I didn't see other children at their house.

Alice's mother was mysteriously and permanently absent. She was either dead or incarcerated in some place where people were sick forever. My mother and grandmother hinted that it was having to live with Miss Rose and Miss Violet that had made her that way. She was sweet and shy, like Alice, but Miss Rose and Miss Violet were mean and bossy to her, and she had had to go away.

"Sisters can destroy a marriage if a man is weak," my mother said to my grandmother. She seemed to say it with deep meaning, and my grandmother nodded.

My father was there. He looked uncomfortable, started to speak, but then didn't. It was unusual for him not to have a comment.

There was the confusing time when my father took me to Sunday School too early. My parents had assumed that the hour for beginning would be the same as it was at home—nine o'clock. So I was let off at the church and went into the Sunday School building while my father drove away.

I opened the door and went into the Sunday School room. There was not a soul there. I sat down on the first row of chairs and waited. Nothing happened. After a while, I got up and walked around the room and stood by the door leading into the next room. There wasn't a sound. I was completely alone, it seemed, in a deserted building.

Finally I decided that the only thing to do was to walk back to Grandmother's house, no matter how long it might take. I wasn't sure of the way, only of the general direction, but surely that would be no problem. My grandparents were known all over town, so anyone could direct me.

I started up the hill from the Presbyterian Church. No one seemed to be out. Finally I saw a woman watering flowers in her front yard.

I paused.

"Do you know the way to Mrs. Henley's house?"

She looked puzzled.

"No, I don't." A slight smile, a small indication of friendliness, but no awareness, no help.

"Oh."

We regarded each other for a moment, neither quite knowing what to do. Then I turned and slowly made my way back to the church. Eventually, I realized, my father was sure to come for me there, even if I had to spend hours in isolation until he arrived. But very shortly after I regained the Sunday School room, the door burst open, letting in sunshine and my friends. They were delighted to see me, and I was surely delighted to see them, so the anxious loneliness evaporated.

There were West Kenyon, a smiling, dark-haired boy in his navy blue suit who always made me feel welcome. And Patty Woodley, a special favorite of mine because she was so much fun. My parents said that her parents were a lot of fun, too, but they were never on time, so her father didn't accomplish as much as he might have in a business way. The Woodleys certainly were fun when I went to Patty's house for lunch, and Mr. Woodley would come home from the office and get us all laughing with his jokes. Maybe he should have been at work then.

Still ahead in those days was the war that would take West into the navy. Patty would go to California and marry him. They would have a few weeks together before he shipped out. Patty stayed in California working, even after his ship went down, even after he was listed as "Missing" and a year later "presumed dead." She kept on waiting after the war was over, hoping he'd turn up. I never knew what happened to her. But none of what was to come intruded on a sunny Sunday. What stayed with me from that day was the wonder at someone who had never heard of my grandmother.

Red-haired Rex was, like me, another sometime-visitor to Atchison. Mother and his mother, Eloise, were first cousins and had been pregnant with us at the same time. So Rex and I were sort of cousins, comfortable and special to each other because we were related but with the extra fillip of not being the same gender. Rex and his parents lived in New Jersey, and sometimes when my father had business in New York, both families met for dinner and some special outing that Rex and I could enjoy.

When our visits to Atchison coincided, Rex and I were delighted. One summer day, Grandmother's then-current maid, Elvira, drove Rex and Mary (where was Martha? I usually saw them together) and me to the country club, planning to leave us there for lunch. Rex had with him a model airplane. Elvira let us out by the club entrance and circled the drive, slowing departing.

"Is she going back now?" Rex asked me.

"Yes."

"I left The Plane in the car!" And he took off after Elvira, while Mary and I stood watching and admiring how fast he ran.

Years away from Atchison, late one Sunday afternoon I answered the telephone in the home I shared with my husband and sons. A deep voice said my name. It was a voice I hadn't heard in years, but it was familiar. It was Rex, in town on business. We directed him to our house, and he was soon at our door.

"Well, you still look like yourself," I said as I greeted him.

"Do I?" he responded and took off his hat. The red hair was

gone, and what was left was white. He suddenly looked remarkably like the pictures of our shared great-grandfather Graham.

At dinner, he told my sons, "Your mother and I are relations who discovered that we liked each other." We still did.

It was less than a year later that I heard that deep voice again through the telephone saying, "...if there's anything I can do...." Somehow I knew it was not an empty offer. I don't know how he knew of my husband's sudden death. Perhaps my uncle had informed him. It seemed right that he should know and hold out his hand. Hesitantly, reluctant to intrude his own happiness on my sorrow, he then told me that he was planning to marry. I was glad for him.

About three years later I traveled to Europe with friends. Rex was being transferred to England and was in London without his wife, arranging for their housing. He called for me at Claridge's one evening, and we went to dinner on the Thames Embankment at a small Italian restaurant. As we sat next to each other on the banquette in the dim room, Rex said, "You remember what I said to you on the telephone." It was a statement, not a question. "... if there's *ever* anything I can do. I meant that."

My fondness for Rex was built on our shared past and extended into our separate futures. In those summer days of childhood, we didn't think of loyalty or our need for strength or comfort. The grown-up world with its unsolvable problems, with its engulfing demands, had not yet intruded.

As Mary and I stood in the hot sunshine, watching Rex running, running after the car, it seemed that all our days were summer ones. If winter were to come, we knew it would bring Christmas.

7

Beyond

Even though after our move to St. Louis I was in Atchison only during vacations, I felt that it was my town. I knew a thrill of recognition and ownership as soon as we crossed the river. Just up that hill, as we turned in the opposite direction for Grandmother's house, was the home of my friend, Ann Bobbie. I would see her soon. We would play on her wide side porch, and her mother, *my* mother's girlhood friend, would serve us lemonade. And I would go out from town to Jackson Park to picnic with my friends and play on the swings and roundabout. I don't recall thinking that the few animals on display were a poor second to our zoo at home. They were familiar friends, to be greeted after absence.

Crossing Commercial Street, I knew that one day soon I would again visit the dry goods store—Grandmother was sure to want to buy yard goods for a dress for me—and I would watch the money she paid be put in a metal cylinder which would run in a little basket on a wire carriage around the ceiling and end, with a tinkling of bells, on the little balcony where the cashier sat, making change. She would put Grandmother's change back in the metal cylinder, and it would repeat the journey in reverse, so that Grandmother could thank the clerk—who thanked *her*—and snap the money back into her big black leather purse.

For many years there were high plank walks in front of the stores on Commercial Street, so high that board steps led down to the street crossings. These were a remnant of the days when customers arrived in buggies or wagons and on horseback. The buildings had overhangs extending partway over the walks. My father showed me the cigar store Indian standing outside the door of a tobacco shop. I liked to look for him. Eventually, though, the store fronts became "modernized," the plank walks paved, the Indian disappeared, and I forgot him.

I knew much from my own experience, but my sense of belonging, of ownership, came from my awareness that Mother's family had helped to build Atchison and were continuing to do so. They had *lived* the town before me. The First Presbyterian Church, where I attended Sunday School, was organized in 1858 in a building on the corner of Second and Commercial Streets owned by Grandmother's Grandfather Eaton. Three years earlier, he had opened the National Hotel on the corner of Second and Atchison Streets. I wondered, when I was old enough to learn of stereotypes, if he had gone into the business because his wife, Varana, was from Switzerland, "the nation of hotel keepers."

If I chanced to spend the day at Bean Lake or Sugar Lake with children of Mother's friends, it was because those friends had cottages on the lakes, cottages where my parents had visited in their courting days. So many of their friends had married before they did. Their social life centered more and more around celebrations of other people's weddings. The married friends acquired the cottages and acted as chaperons for the unmarried ones, of whom my parents sometimes seemed the last survivors.

And if—oh, glory!—the circus came to town when I was there, I would stand with my father on Commercial Street as the clowns and elephants passed, just as my mother remembered doing in her childhood. She also remembered other parades, the parades of the

Parade float

flowers, when floats were covered with flowers from family gardens, and she and her brother, Graham, dressed up and sober, would drive the pony cart led by an equally dressed-up black attendant.

Uncle Graham wasn't always so cooperative as a child. Mother still had a trace of smug superiority when she recalled how she and Graham were taken by their mother to call on a woman friend. Uncle Graham was dressed up in a sailor suit, which he didn't like. Great-grandmother's carriage, usually at their disposal, was engaged that afternoon, and Grandmother had to take both children by trolley. Uncle Graham wouldn't get on. Mother said he screamed and kicked, and Grandmother had to lift him on, a feat I could not imagine. And then when they got to the woman's house, she gave them a cool drink each in a crystal glass, and Uncle Graham *took a bite out of the glass*! Mother said Grandmother had to buy the woman a new glass.

The mill, bearing my great-grandfather's name and headed during most of my childhood by my uncle Graham (who never bit glasses any more), was one focal point of the town. Sometimes my uncle took me into the open grain-storage rooms and gave me raw wheat to chew. He said it was better than gum. The mill workers in their flour-dusty overalls and peak-brimmed caps would smile indulgently and scoop more wheat from the open sacks if I wanted it. Everything seemed very clean. Perhaps it was the white flour sifted everywhere that made it seem so.

I was in Atchison the summer the grain elevator burned and the mill buildings caught fire too. Spontaneous combustion, with all of that packed grain and the Kansas heat? If anyone ever knew, I didn't find out. The town turned out to watch the blaze spread. There was no hope of control. My uncle Graham and Uncle Cyrus Blake, who managed the elevator, stood silent, shirt-sleeved and helpless on the sidewalk as the equally helpless fireman sprayed the too-short plumes of water at the leaping flames. Weeks after we came home, Grandmother would write, "The elevator is still burning."

The fire smoldered in the enclosed granary, feeding on itself. There was no way to extinguish the sparks without ruining the grain. How such a catastrophe might hurt the business and the family never entered my head. Nothing seemed to change.

Dr. Charley, forever the family's doctor, it seemed, made part of the familiar scene for me. He seemed nearly always to show up at Grandmother's house during my visits. Grandfather was sure to call him when he felt anxious about Grandmother. Tall, spare, cadaverous with his deep, hollow voice and long, cold fingers that

The flour mill on fire

handled his stethoscope, he would appear, calm in the face of Grandfather's distraction. He was always unruffled, if outspoken. People liked to quote his sayings, even when his bluntness shocked them.

Once, called to the bedside of an elderly, ailing woman, he silently performed his examination. "Well, Charley," said her son-in-law, attempting to relieve the tension with a light tone, "what would you say was wrong with her?" And Dr. Charley, replacing the stethoscope, drawled, "Not a damn thing. She's just going to die. That's all." He was right.

No one in Atchison ever thought of Dr. Charley dying. After all, he had served four generations, starting his practice with his father. It was to distinguish him from old Dr. Nelson that he had become Dr. Charley. But one spring day, in his usual leisurely manner, he sauntered down Commercial Street to the post office. He accomplished his business and turned to go. The clerk saw him fall. He was dead before anyone reached him.

The town was stunned. Grandmother was, I think, surprised to find that she continued to live without Dr. Charley. He had never been ill. Tall, gaunt, and stoop-shouldered, he had looked the same for as long as anyone could remember. He knew his heart was weak—had known as a young man and had decided, therefore, not to pursue a career in surgery, though he was said to be brilliant at it. A few months before his death his office building on Seventh Street had caught fire, and he had crawled down the stairs on his hands and knees to avoid the smoke. His old heart had carried him through that time, but couldn't survive buying a stamp.

The auction at Dr. Charley's house let Atchison people in where they were never invited during his lifetime. After the death of his mother, he had spent little time at his home, or at any other. He turned down all invitations to meals—("Won't you stay to dinner, Dr. Charley?" Grandmother would invite from her sickbed, while I begged, "Oh, yes, *please*, Dr. Charley!")—insisting he "only ate to live." He was most comfortable in his office, where the light shone late at night. His will, showing assets of over a hundred thousand dollars during those depression years, was found stuffed in the pocket of an old raincoat hung on a peg in his office. What he might have been worth, no one knew, for he sent out bills only once a year, on the first of January.

The house in which he lived, first with his parents then alone, had taken on his appearance. Both were old-fashioned, plain, with an air of frugality. The dark, unblinking windows stared with the same silent judgement as the deep-sunken, slightly-protruding eyes of the doctor.

I went with Mother and much of the town to the auction. People poured into the spare old house, clucking over the possessions that must have been accumulated by his spendthrift mother, whom he adored and pampered after his father's death. Priceless first editions and morocco-bound volumes, never unwrapped, were stacked in the library. While people wandered about below, I climbed the stairs and looked until I found the bedroom that must have been Dr. Charley's. The bed was stripped, and the curtains had been removed. But perhaps the room had always looked so bare. I opened the closet door.

Nothing was in the closet, except for one item. Hanging on a hook was one limp, gray shirt. Instantly, I could see Dr. Charley with his high stiff collars, his high-topped shoes, his suits of either brown or a rusty gray-tan, and always a gray shirt. That limp shirt, placed there by those long cold fingers which had last unbuttoned the buttons and released the collar button from the back of the neck, that shirt reproached me for my invasion. Shamed, I closed the door.

Mother was pleased to find some dessert plates which matched a set that had been Great-grandmother's. She bought them so that she now had enough alike for a good-sized party.

Like Dr. Charley's, Grandfather's office was up a flight of stairs in one of the buildings on a block running off Commercial Street. The room where Miss Hortense, his secretary, sat had a long narrow table in the center. Here she neatly stacked the magazines about insurance and investments which had to do with Grandfather's business. Miss Hortense was always welcoming to me, implying that I was someone special, an attitude that Grandfather gruffly encouraged.

Grandfather had left the bank years ago, shortly after Mother came home from Miss Bennet's Boarding School. I was never clear as to the reasons for his leaving, probably because I was more

acceptive of the present than curious about the past. A few times
Mother or Grandmother would mention with a sense of long-ago
injustice a Mr. Somebody who had worked with Grandfather and
made things difficult, so difficult that Grandfather got sick and
couldn't work for a year. No one quite said "nervous breakdown,"
because Grandfather was known to be so "well-balanced." A time
or two, in my presence, Grandfather said he had the best wife in
the world, who had stood by him during his illness. Whether the
difficulty had anything to do with the loan which Grandfather
approved for an Oklahoma farmer was never mentioned. The
farmer defaulted, the bank took over the farm, and Grandfather
was so conscience-stricken that he repaid the money to the bank,
which turned the property over to him. So he ended with chagrin
at his mistaken judgement, concern for the farmer, and a worthless
Oklahoma farm, which he rented out. Eventually, after the farm
passed into his estate, there was talk of oil and gas rights, but none
of that helped Grandfather.

During that year of illness, Uncle Edgar appeared with his private
railroad car and carried Grandfather off on a trip to Mexico. Perhaps
the trip worked a cure. Or perhaps those two very private men
were able to talk to each other in their secluded surroundings.
Perhaps, with his brother's advice, Grandfather decided on a new
career. He was certainly respected around town and was known as
a capable, upright man, so the bank episode, whatever it was, did
not hurt his reputation.

A more extensive office, reached by a cagelike elevator, was that
of the eye, ear, nose and throat specialist, Dr. Bach. Of German
heritage and training, he was a no-nonsense physician. During the
era when tonsilectomies were popular, he sat my parents upright
in his office chair and, in turn, removed their tonsils—without
anesthesia. I remember them smiling bravely into bloody hand-
kerchiefs afterwards, while I was silently grateful for my hospital

stay in St. Louis for the same operation. Having already had my tonsils out, I could safely, if cautiously, like Dr. Bach without having to prove my bravery.

Summer evenings, to cool off we often took a ponderous ride in the current Hudson, out "the Effingham road," perhaps. Grandfather, with a connoisseur's tone, would comment on the state of the corn which we passed. People encouraged themselves during the hot, dry summer by saying, "It's good corn weather." Once, because I had spied a tumble-down log cabin in a field, he and I trudged over the stubble so that I could lay my hand on the derelict wall and recite as much as I could remember of a poem called "The House with Nobody In It." I had read it in *Silver Pennies*, a volume of poetry for children, and more or less memorized it. Mother and Grandmother waited in the car. Grandfather stood patiently without comment and couldn't have known if I had left out some lines.

Shorter drives were apt to take us up "the Orphan's Home Road," and we would slowly circle the grounds of the home while I looked for orphans. Sometimes we would wave to each other. But some of the bigger orphans only glared. I couldn't understand why.

In the same direction but nearer to Grandmother's house was the Blue House. It was really a rather shabby frame house, probably lived in by some poor but spirited people. In a world of white frame or stucco, they had painted their house gloriously sky blue. I had never seen such a thing and reported it to my friends at home. If I took a walk by myself in that direction, I made sure to go as far as the Blue House.

All of my forays into the comfortingly familiar ended always in the haven of Grandmother's house. It was the safe *known*, where I too was known and knew myself. I didn't realize that I was always within boundaries, that there was one place where I didn't go. And I didn't dream that there was, not very far away, a place where I would be neither welcomed nor accepted.

8

The Other Grandmother

Everyone has two grandmothers. I knew that, of course. But for me "Grandmother" meant my mother's mother, the one who lived in Atchison in the house where my mother had been a little girl. She was the grandmother who helped me roll out cookies at the oilcloth-covered kitchen table and let me select the new pattern when the old oilcloth cracked and needed to be replaced. When I wasn't there to help with the production, she sent me sugar cookies packed in a dress box, cut in marvelous shapes, and arriving, miraculously intact, to be opened in our kitchen in Kirkwood, Missouri. She made me dresses and doll clothes on the treadle sewing machine set up in the sunny bay window in Grandfather's bedroom.

She brushed my hair in sausage curls around her finger when Mother wasn't there (it was the Dutch-bob era for children). She showed me a lock of her own little-girl hair carefully wrapped in tissue paper. It had been shorn from her head one hot summer day when her well-meaning father had been walking with her downtown in Atchison. "Mr. Graham, your little girl looks so hot," said the barber lounging at his shop door. "Why don't you bring her in, and we'll cut that heavy hair?" My great-grandfather, always a hail-fellow and unaware of the nuances of feminine values, thought that a fine idea. Grandmother told me how she watched her curls cover the floor and cried in the barber chair.

When they got home, her outraged mother explained quite clearly why the idea was *not* fine, using words like "woman's crowning glory." For a long time I envisioned my grandmother as nearly bald from the age of five, with only one salvaged curl for solace. She showed me how similar in color it was to mine.

So a grandmother was someone who loved you and of whom you were a part, clearly definable, separated only by time.

"I have *two* grandmothers," said my friend. We were eight-year-olds bouncing in the back seat of our Oakland car, driven by my mother on one of those jaunts that mothers of grade-schoolers undertake. "*One* grandmother is here in St. Louis, and *one* grandmother is in Oklahoma."

"*I* have two grandmothers, too." I was not going to come up short. "One grandmother is in Atchison, Kansas, and the other is in Atchison, too, but we never go to see her." The puzzle slowly presented itself. "Mother, why don't we ever go to see her?"

"Ellen, be quiet!" said my mother in a strange, sharp tone. My friend and I exchanged glances, and I shrugged at the inexplicable ways of grown-ups.

My parents believed in dealing with children's problems promptly. Soon after that incident, we were in the waiting room of the big depot in Kansas City, between trains to Atchison on a visit to my grandparents, my comfortably identifiable grandparents, *my* grandparents. My father crossed to where I was sitting on the long varnished wooden bench. Mother stayed across the aisle, a very wide one it seemed, but I could feel her watching.

My father, his hat at its usual conservatively jaunty angle, his mouth slightly smiling under the mustache but his eyes serious, sat down beside me. He began to talk in the tone he always used to explain things, as if I were a grown-up and would understand. "I love my mother just as you love your mother," he said. There was a light haze of stale cigarette smoke in the air, the blurred bustle of many persons just at the periphery of our notice, the shine of the varnished benches. I glanced across at my mother. She looked tense. "But when we married, my mother said I couldn't bring my wife to her home. So, naturally, I couldn't go. Because I chose to love your mother first. So I can't go to see my mother, and neither can you."

He kept giving me that look which required me to understand. And I did understand. Of course, if one had to choose between my mother and someone else—anyone, particulary a faceless person unimaginable to me—one would choose my mother. If not— if he had chosen otherwise—he would have chosen that I would never be. The explanation satisfied me for the time. It was only much later that I began to realize that I didn't understand at all.

Once the subject was opened, my mother and even my grandmother told me more. My father never talked about it again. His stories of his mother and sister, the only remaining members of his original family, were all of the early days before he became a lawyer and the family moved to Atchison to establish his practice. They were stories of a houseful of pets, of many cousins, of Christmas celebrations, and of his Danish father who died when my father was ten.

Mother told the dark part. The mother and sister were mean and unnatural people. At first when my parents began to see each other, my father would sometimes include his sister in their trips to the theater. She was very pleasant to Mother then. "But as soon as she saw that Daddy was serious about me, she changed." The mother and daughter combined to block the marriage.

"Why were they like that?"

"Jealous," said my mother. "They wanted Daddy all to themselves. They didn't want him to marry *anyone*."

And they were jealous that Mother's family were town leaders, and they were new arrivals, appearing, fatherless, a widow, her daughter, and a son with a new law degree in hand. My Danish grandfather had owned a saloon in Carrollton, Missouri. My father had always said his father was "in real estate." But my Presbyterian grandfather checked and found the other story. When he faced my father with the damning truth, my father, as Mother later told it, "tried to say the saloon was only payment for a bad debt." I was a shade disappointed that my grandfather would investigate my father that way. It didn't seem quite fair.

After my parents married, my aunt and other grandmother became recluses, my mother said. Adelia (my aunt, nicknamed "Dud," the word for a bomb that never went off, my mother pointed out) had been a beautiful young woman, but she "let herself get fat," said my thin mother. She had attended the university when my father had, majoring in Greek, but never did anything with her education. She liked children and could have taught school but didn't. A wasted, empty life.

They lived in a square red brick house on Fourth Street. My mother pointed it out to me. There was no sign of life, though it was meticulously kept. The oval glass of the front door curtained, the shades pulled down, giving the windows a sightless stare, the house sat on a low terrace. The stories were that they ordered their groceries by telephone but wouldn't answer the door when the delivery boy came. Instead they let down a basket on a rope from an upstairs window and pulled the food up.

One early morning as we drove to the railroad station to go home, I caught sight of a dark-haired woman rocking on the front porch. Mother sniffed as we drove by. Later she told me in hushed tones (though no one else could have heard) that *she* was my father's sister. "She only comes out when there's no one around." Like my father, she must have been an early riser.

Whenever we passed after that, I looked, hoping to see someone, but I never did. I always said to myself, "My grandmother lives there. And my Aunt Dud."

Sometimes, my mother told me, my father would come home sighing. "I heard from Atchison today." Mother said it was always a vitriolic letter. He sent them money, I was told. But when I went through his safe deposit box after his death and found the cancelled checks, I was surprised they represented so little money. Of course, he could have given them stocks or other assets. I hope he did.

Mother said he had made one final effort to heal the breach. Still with the bitterness born of the long-ago rejection of a generous gesture that she must have reluctantly agreed to during a somewhat pinched time, she told me of his attempt that first Christmas of my life. It was not an affluent time for my parents. My father's law career, only just begun at the start of World War I, had been disrupted by his service as a naval aviator. He was struggling to establish himself and to support his new family. But he fixed a basket of delicacies which he knew his mother and sister enjoyed and sent them with a letter. Wasn't this a time to overlook the past? Wouldn't they come to see the baby?

Mother told me his letter crossed with a letter they sent him— a particularly vituperative letter. He had made his last overture.

9

Nostrums and Nourishment

Ranking along with God and the Presbyterian minister (who were usually indistinguishable) in Grandmother's regard was The Doctor. Directives from any of the three were to be obeyed without question. When they conflicted, The Doctor won out.

In the matter of the eggnog, The Doctor—or maybe Grandmother—was the clear winner. As she grew older, which she did for a long time since she lived for eighty-seven years, Grandmother's energy and appetite diminished. The Doctor suggested that she have an afternoon eggnog as a light supplementary nourishment. Such refreshment was fine with Grandmother, and tall glasses of creamy foam, daintily served on a silver tray with an embroidered linen tea napkin (cocktails were unheard of in that house) were sent daily to Grandmother's bedroom. She dutifully drained them.

Then The Doctor had another idea. "I would suggest," he said on one of his calls, "that you add a little apricot brandy to your eggnog. It would—ah—increase your energy."

Apricot brandy was alcohol, and God and the Presbyterian Church were foresquare against consuming alcohol. Yet here was a statement from The Doctor, whose pronouncements were as weighty as those from Mount Sinai. Grandmother protested, as does the young girl who feels a pro forma "No" is required before the "Yes" she means to give. My uncle, who was tacitly understood to know such things, though it was never acknowledged that he drank, was dispatched to purchase the bottle of brandy. Grandfather, the treasurer of the local Presbyterian Church ultimately for fifty years, obviously couldn't go into a liquor store. Anyway, the state of Kansas didn't have liquor stores. My uncle, though, knew where to go—across the bridge to the Missouri side, where, just on the river's edge, in sin and prosperity, the appropriate store stood.

The apricot brandy came into the house. The day for its first use was known. Grandmother made a big fuss, but agreed to take her medicine. One teaspoonful of brandy was added to the big ice tea glass of eggnog. Everyone stood around to watch Grandmother drink. She took a sip. She made a face. She gagged. She drank it all.

By the end of the week, Grandmother was sending her eggnog back to the kitchen. The help seemed to forget to put in her apricot brandy, and some had to be added each afternoon. "Grandmother's so *good* about taking her eggnog!" said my mother.

Grandmother wasn't a complete layman when it came to medical matters. After all, she had a brother who was a doctor. Having a doctor in the family, especially one who was grateful for the financial support she had offered during his training, was convenient. After the birth of my uncle Graham, their second child, Grandfather declared he would never "put her through that again" because she had been so sick. Uncle Ed told him how *not* to put her through it. In the 1890s, not everyone had such useful knowledge right in the family.

Being related to a medical degree that way gave Grandmother and Great-grandmother a feeling of authority in matters of health.

Great-grandmother chewed every bite thirty times as an aid to digestion. I often wondered how she kept count. Did she forego all conversation at meals in order to concentrate?

Grandmother had her own beliefs. My visits often seemed to coincide with new discoveries which I was required to practice. I remember her salt-and-baking soda mixture for teeth-brushing, harmless enough, I suppose, and even effective, but rather a nuisance to put together and certainly messy. The powder kept escaping all over the brown marble sink as I brushed. Then there was the period when Grandmother espoused drinking a full glass of warm water with lemon juice before breakfast. I can remember standing at that same brown marble basin and laboriously swallowing. This practice was to encourage proper "elimination."

"Elimination" was a subject of great importance. My daily success or failure was to be reported to an adult. There was a prescribed time of day for this endeavor, *right* after breakfast. It was important to "establish good habits." My well-meaning mother and grandmother, each schooled in a generation in which a lady stayed properly in her home until midmorning, could never have anticipated that midtwentieth century horror, the breakfast conference, or how much discomfort those good habits have caused.

Surely I wasn't given a dose of mineral oil *every* night at Grandmother's house, but the procedure seemed to be a part of going to bed. The bottle stood on the window sill in the butler's pantry, so the oil was usually a little cool. The cake, left over from the afternoon's callers or from dinner, sat on the counter in front of the window. I could lift the domed cover and cut myself as big a piece as I wished for my reward.

"Stay six feet away from anyone with a cold," admonished Grandmother. "The germs can't travel more than six feet." She was always reading things like that in The Paper. The Paper was equal to the

Bible in authority. Unfortunately, somebody always threw The Paper away before anyone else could read Grandmother's articles. But even today, if I don't stop myself, I find myself backing up and measuring with my eye the distance between me and someone with a cold.

Never at a loss for a remedy or a prevention, Grandmother spared no expense when she suspected an emergency. During World War I my mother joined my father after he was commissioned as a naval aviator. They were stationed in Boston when the flu epidemic struck. Grandmother, far away in the Midwest, could not protect her family. But she recognized her challenge and her duty. She dispatched a telegrammed command to my parents. In its entirety it read: "USE LISTERINE FREELY."

My father used to tell that story with whoops of laughter. I supposed it was amusing, but more than that it proved to me that Grandmother could cope with anything. Anyway, my parents never did get the flu.

"When I was a boy in Pennsylvania," said Grandfather, standing to attack the Sunday roast, "there was a man had a store. I went there with my father sometimes. He had everything you could think of in that store. But he had a sign over the front counter, and it said: 'If you don't see what you want, ask for it.' So *you* do that, Topsy." He gestured over the table with the carving knife. "If you don't see what you want, ask for it."

Grandmother, who was, after all, in charge of what went on the table, waited until this declaration of hospitality was complete. Then she said, "Harry, you're dripping on the tablecloth."

Grandfather's drips while serving were a great trial to Grandmother and the maid, necessitating a clean cloth for every meal. Finally they devised the system of placing damask napkins at Grandfather's end of the table to catch the inevitable spills between serving dish and plate. Grandfather was a little shamefaced, but acquiescent. He knew his shortcomings.

I can't imagine that I ever thought of anything to ask for. That table was bountifully provided, without my thought or effort, with everything necessary for my well-being and pleasure. I don't remember that even the things that were good for me were distasteful. Never did I have to face, as I did at home, a soggy green-gray brussels sprout.

Atchison was full of good cooks, and Grandmother and Great-grandmother were among the best. They had recipes with their names on them in the *Junior-Senior League Cook Book*, which stated that it included "many carefully guarded culinary secrets that have made Atchison hostesses famous," and in the cookbooks "published by the Ladies of the Presbyterian Church."

The *Junior-Senior League Cook Book* had a foreword describing the purpose of the publication as two-fold: " . . . to make known the favorite recipes of Atchison's best cooks, and to raise money for the Public Health and the League's private charities." Loyal husbands and sons, who were also local businessmen and merchants who hoped to retain the ladies as customers, bought advertisements in the book. "As always, without the help of Atchison merchants, the League's plans for assisting Atchison's dependents would have been far less successful," the League's foreword stated, acknowledging the "cheerful cooperation" of the advertisers.

The ads themselves were cheerful and upbeat, ranging from a succinct "Best Things to Eat" from Childress's Grocery to more detailed information: a poultry company offered not only poultry but "Gasoline and Oils for Less"; the Ice Company recommended: "Save with Ice—Ice-Freshened Food Looks Better—Tastes Better and Is Better. Ice is Inexpensive. Use it Generously—for Better

Appetite and Better Health." The Power and Light Company urged slyly: "Women who use automatic cookery . . . have time to take advantage of afternoon social invitations."

The Graham Milling Company, of *course*, took a full-page ad, touting its "certified kitchen products" which were said to be "time-savers and insure perfect cooking results." As an apparent antidote to any possibly disastrous results, fifteen doctors of the Atchison County Medical Society also took a full-page ad, offering their "compliments." And a legal firm, in a discreet third of a page, stated "If you are entitled to a divorce on account of bad cooking we might get it for you, tho we do not like the divorce business."

Grandmother evidently wasn't much interested in the ads, for she pasted more recipes over many of them. But the pages of recipes, her friends and her own, got her full attention. There was Grandmother's recipe for marble cake, a mixture of two separate doughs, one white and one tan. The tan part was made with spices, brown sugar and molasses. Butter the "size of a hickory nut" was an ingredient of cream pie, and Great-grandmother called for a "teacupful" of milk and the same of powdered sugar in her lemon custard. Although Grandmother generously gave credit where it was due ("This is Madge Burrows' apple cake," she might say), she was selective with her approval. "Not good. Too sweet!" she wrote over one recipe, her rejection so complete that none of the directions could thereafter be read.

Any flour called for in those recipes was, of course, Graham's Certified Flour from the mill. The large flour sacks stood in the cool storage pantry. They were made of flower-sprigged cloth. Grandmother said that my uncle had the material printed in patterns because the farmers' wives like to make dresses from the sacks.

Although my father complained about the gravy at Grand-mother's house, saying it was made of burned flour, I never found anything to criticize. Her special dishes never tasted so good any-

where else, even when Mother made them at home. At Christmas
or Thanksgiving, cranberry frappe, served in tall sherbet glasses,
accompanied the main course. When you felt clogged with turkey
and dressing, a cold, tart spoonful of frappe revived your will to
eat. In the summer the produce was fresh from nearby farms and
gardens. Grandmother always sprinkled sugar over the ripe tomato
slices, so I did too.

On many summer afternoons I went with Grandmother to visit
the tomato women. They had wooden stands under shady trees in
their front yards. The vegetable gardens were out back. I would
be up from a rest in the Blue Bedroom, bathed and freshly dressed
in dimity or dotted swiss or organdy. If Grandmother had made
my dress, it was probably yellow or orange or apricot.

"Is this your granddaughter, Mrs. Henley?" the tomato women
would ask as they put the tomatoes or the just-picked corn or the
string beans into brown paper bags.

"Yes, this is my granddaughter from St. Louis."

"My! Did you come alone?"

"No. I came with my mother." (But I wished from then on that
I could have said, "Yes. Yes. I got on the train and I came *all by
myself*.")

Sometimes there would be something special to see, a cat to
stroke perhaps. And I would go away happy and content and tell
Grandfather about the cat at dinner.

Grandfather had his own specialties. I went with him on Saturday mornings when the farmers set up their stalls next to the
station. Everyone we passed seemed to know Grandfather. Men
said, "Hello, Mr. Henley," and tipped their hats to him. We might
take the maid with us. Grandfather would park the big Hudson
in the shade, and while the maid foraged for corn or whatever
Grandmother had specified, Grandfather and I would go for the

cantaloupe. Grandfather was an acknowledged cantaloupe expert. He never picked out a bad one. Whenever we had cantaloupe, it was Grandfather who chose it.

"That one," he would say, standing before the cantaloupe stand. "That one." Not imperiously, but with no false humility either. Then when we ate it, the comments at the table were, "Father certainly knows how to choose a cantaloupe." "Father never chooses a bad one."

Once we went to eat strawberries off the vine, Mother, Grandmother, and I. I was dressed in a white dress, because stains wash out of white best. We crawled in leisurely fashion up and down the rows, and there was the smell of dust and sun and peace and the feel of a white clapboard house somewhere behind us. It was the safe time, the summertime.

10

The Other Side

Atchison was childhood, but the best of childhood. I don't remember ever being unhappy or embarrassed there. Childhood isn't uniformly happy, even at best, but in Atchison I had a feeling that I didn't always have at home. Everything was all right.

I was all right, too. Not that I was considered perfect, but the expectation was that I was perfectible. All it took was guidance and time. There were standards, but I would attain them. Once when I was chasing a butterfly in the front yard I cried out, "I touched him!"

"You *what*?" said my grandfather, watching from the front porch.

"I touched him."

"Oh." Mollified. "I thought you said you 'catched' him." The latent schoolteacher in him was ever alert to my grammar.

And once, when I was trying to sweep something, Grandfather became indignant that I didn't know how to use a broom properly. He took it from me and showed me how. I was a bit abashed, but the clear implication was that my mother should have taught me. It was her failure, not mine.

Not so at home. "That's about a B," my father would say scornfully of some performance of mine, academic or otherwise, that didn't please him. Or, "Why not an A?" on the occasions that I paused at a B +. "Why do you suppose they have A's if you're not supposed to get them?" Once I argued that the same could be said about C's, D's, and F's, but my logic did not appeal to him. A good lawyer, he accepted only his own conclusions and argued from them.

"I'd give a hundred dollars if you could run like that," he once said, observing a younger child sprint ahead of us on a woodland path. I had never given any thought to how I ran, but clearly I didn't satisfy my father's standards, and the implication was that I never would.

"You're not remembering to rub Vaseline on your eyebrows at night, are you?" he said. "That will darken them. I don't like people with blond eyebrows." Despairingly, I peered in the mirror at my offending feature that night and rubbed some petroleum jelly on them. I had never thought about my eyebrows before, but there they were, sticking out of my face for everyone to see and judge. If my father didn't like me because of their color, the whole world must be judging me the same way.

He had played tennis, and, viewing the cups he had won, I supposed he never lost. One day when I was perhaps eight, he came home with a present for me. It was a special-sized tennis racket which he had had made for me. He had had it strung with red, white and blue gut, and he told me that it cost sixty dollars. That was a lot of money in those days, especially since I had never shown the slightest interest in tennis. But I was supposed to be grateful. And he would teach me. We went to the country club court, and my father showed me how to hold the racket, and how to swing. Then he stood across the net from me and began serving me balls. I didn't hit a one. I could feel my father being patient, but that didn't last long. When finally we came home to my apprehensive mother, it was in failure and despair.

Ever a tenacious man, my father decided that a professional teacher, while certainly not as skilled as he, might have more success in teaching me. Dutifully I lugged my racket in its special press to the Northern resort where we vacationed. I had a few lessons, but my father said that practice was the thing I needed, so I should practice while the rest of them went to the beach. For two hours I doggedly swatted balls at a green wooden backstop. The place was deserted. I don't think I ever managed to return more than three balls in a row, but I kept at it. Finally, the requisite time accomplished, I joined the family at the beach. My mother looked at me anxiously as I lay down in the sand and covered my eyes with my hand.

"You look so hot. Don't you want to swim?"

"No. I have a headache."

No one said anything. I lay with my eyes closed, but I could feel a look pass between my parents. Finally my father said, "Are you practicing tennis just to please me?"

Ordinarily, I would have given an answer to please him. But I was so exhausted, so hot, so in despair about my own permanent— it seemed—lack of skill that I was honest. "Yes," I said.

A short silence and another exchanged look. Then, "You don't have to play tennis anymore if you really don't want to," said my father.

"Thank you."

He may have been hoping for another answer, but he didn't show it. It wasn't that he was an unkind man. I think it was only that, having just one child, he wanted that child to be everything, scholar, athlete, actress, writer, school leader, and withal loved and beautiful. I have sometimes marveled that he didn't urge me to go out for football. When I was born, my uncle teased him, "Well, a girl can't be a tackle."

To which my father replied, "Well, a boy can't dance ballet."

I didn't do that, either. Perhaps if he had had a son, that boy would have been a dancer. I couldn't have equaled such a disaster.

But the worst times were the arithmetic lessons. Ever involved in my school work, my father soon was convinced that I was learning no mathematics at all. The books were all wrong. He knew the book I needed. With his characteristic Germanic diligence, he scoured the second-hand book stores along Market Street in St. Louis. Progress reports were made at dinner, while I silently hoped that every copy of his childhood text had crumbled into dust. I was doomed, of course, to his inevitable triumph. One night he proudly brandished a miserable little brown-on-brown volume, Milne's *Standard Arithmetic*. All through dinner he chatted happily about the wonders which we would explore together. My food sat cold and lumpy in my churning stomach.

After dinner—immediately after—my father settled himself comfortably in his chair. I was stationed behind it, to look over his shoulder. My nose just cleared the high back, which I have since determined was thirty-eight inches high. With relish, my father opened the book to what he deemed the appropriate place and began to read aloud with great clarity. We tackled the "word problems." They all seemed to be about odiously industrious boys who, separately or together, mowed an endless series of lawns, and how long would it take them to do the job either way? My father read the final question. Silence from me. Across the room, my mother concentrated on her darning.

Again, my father read the problem and the question, patience dripping from his voice. "I'm not asking you for the answer. How do you *think* you would go about solving the problem?"

An almost inaudible, "I don't know," from me. The smell of the mohair filled my nostrils. My mother darned faster. My father became more testily patient. Once more, we read about the lawn mowers. Inhaling the aroma of mohair, I hadn't the faintest idea as to how to begin. My father was talking about something called algebra, and how simple that made everything. He began to show me how easy the solution became, making *x*'s and = marks on some of the same paper that he used for his briefs.

"*Now* you see, don't you?"

I didn't, not at all.

The sessions always ended in the same way. My father would explode, my mother would remain silent, and I would flee up the stairs in tears. Then, after a time of murmured conversation between my parents, my father would mount the stairs, enter my darkened room and sit on the edge of my bed. I don't recall what he said. There was never an apology or a retraction of his position. It was just that somehow we made up. But that didn't erase my feeling of failure. Nor did the fact that I made good grades in school and had some double promotions, being allowed to skip grades. No teacher ever suggested that I needed extra work in arithmetic. But that just proved how little *they* knew. My father proved how little I knew. And I know just that amount to this day.

But in Atchison I was approved. Grandmother was delighted when I was there, Grandfather was watchfully protective and played a game to see who could do best at eating oatmeal. I won. My friends were glad to see me, their mothers were reasonably admiring, and no one ever commented that my eyebrows were too light.

The only time that I ever encountered disapproval, at least that I recall, was once when my uncle, distraught that his wife had been taken to Kansas City for surgery, spanked my little cousin for crying. Graham, Jr. howled louder.

"Of *course* he'll cry if you spank him," I said scornfully, and my uncle answered, "*Ordinarily* I don't mind what you do, Ellen."

Miffed, I subsided. Much as I wanted approval, *everyone*'s approval, I was secure in my feeling of injustice. My uncle was wrong, so his displeasure with me wasn't my fault. It didn't count.

There was, of course, the incident at Jack Blake's birthday party when I was about three years old. It was my first party with big children. I'm not sure why Jack's mother, whom I called Aunt Mildred, included me, because everyone else was a member of Jack's class, which had just concluded the first grade. I remember the whole class being led down the hill by their teacher, who had been my uncle Graham's teacher, too. I stood with Jack and his older sister, Betty Ann, to watch what seemed to be an endless line of children approach.

While we were all wandering around in some disorder out of doors, one of the big girls noticed a gold bracelet I was wearing. I always wore it; my uncle Graham had given it to me. The big girl wanted it, and when I refused, she slapped me.

I didn't know what to do. I had been taught to bring unsolvable problems to my parents, but they weren't there. I thought the next best substitutes were any available adults, so I went into the house where the teacher sat with Aunt Mildred and some other mothers. I reported the slap. Aunt Mildred laughed indulgently. "Oh, you'll have to get used to that when you go to school," she said.

I didn't want to go to school.

When I came back outside, Jack was talking to the girl who had slapped me. He seemed cross. His black eyebrows were pulled together, and he was speaking with great emphasis. "She's only a *little* kid," I heard him say. "You shouldn't hit little kids." My tormentor stood staring at him, looking as if she might cry herself. Jack seemed to relent. "Anyway, we need you for this next game," he said. "So come on." The slap seemed to vanish. I didn't even mind what had happened, if that brought Jack to my defense.

∴ ∴ ∴

The schedule at Grandmother's house seemed set by benign adults for my enjoyment, and was as much the scheme of things as sunrise and sunset. I had no feeling of imposed discipline, but rather of a freedom to explore—the house, the yard, and time itself. A child alone, dependent largely on my own devices, I read the books, dressed up in the clothes, slept in the beds, handled the artifacts of an age before my birth. The latter Victorian years were preserved in Grandmother's house, and I tasted their flavor a generation and more after their end.

The magic of my entry into another lifetime made all places in Grandmother's house special. But the best spots were where no one else was, the secret places that were mine. The grape arbor on the kitchen porch was one such place. There was a seat along the porch railing, and the grape vines trellised up to the ceiling, making a leafy bower through which the sun filtered. I watched the green grapes begin to form. Usually I had gone home by the time they purpled, and Grandmother made grape jelly which she sent to us. But there was always jelly from last year to be served with the hot rolls made from Graham's Certified Flour. The jelly I liked best had a thin sugary layer on top. The jar sat in a handpainted container, a Bavarian fantasy of pink and green flowers and gilt swirls on a cream ground.

The grape arbor wasn't a perfect special place, too close as it was to the kitchen window and the long oilcloth-covered table beneath it. Here the rolls were formed, the cookies cut out, and while conversations through the kitchen window were pleasant enough, they intruded on my world of pretend.

The basement was better. You entered the basement through a large, hard-to-manage wooden door under the kitchen porch. In the summer, tendrils from the grape vines, which were twined on the porch lattice above, would have impeded closing the door if anyone had wanted to do so. Mostly it stood propped open so that the laundry could easily be brought up the stairs and hung outdoors on the wire clothes lines wrapped around the tall pine trees. Or, they *were* wire until one summer night lightning hit the line, ran along it to the nearest pine, and shattered the tree.

When you went down the short flight of steps into the cool basement corridor, at first you couldn't see. Partly that was because you were sunblind, but the corridor was shadowy, lit only by the light that filtered through the lattice on one side. A high ledge held old flower pots and other items saved, half-forgotten but potentially valuable. I understand Grandmother's habit. I do the same thing.

You began to get the dank basement smell as soon as you entered the corridor. That corridor led to my favorite room, the laundry room. The basement was divided into four or five rooms with corridors between. Most were dusky and still floored with hard-packed dirt through which bedrock protruded in places, making footing unsteady in the half dark.

But the laundry room could have been a place to live! The floor was brick, like the floor of the main corridor. The stone foundation walls were whitewashed, and because this area was under the library bay window, it, too, had a sunny three-windowed bay. The panes were set close to the ceiling. You could see only the legs and feet of the iceman or the boy from Childress' Grocery as they made deliveries to the kitchen. The sinks and tubs were under the bay, and in the center of the room stood an iron stove for the big washtubs in which the clothes were boiled. On laundry days the room smelled of steam and starch and ironed clothes as Florence, the laundress, put clothes through the wringer and changed a cooling iron for a hot one as she worked on the crisp linen sheets, the damask tablecloths, my dresses with matching bloomers.

A door led from the laundry room to an inner room, shadowy and private. Into the panel of the door were scratched the words

"Graham Henley Ofic," remnant of my uncle's boyhood activity. When I asked him what he had used the office for, he couldn't remember. I looked for his sign every visit, feeling a little superior over his misspelling.

And one year there were kittens in the basement. A mother cat had come in the coal-chute window and had fortuitously delivered just before one of my visits. Grandmother hated cats but was temporarily forbearing for my amusement. Daily I maneuvered the treacherous angled stairs from the kitchen and found my way through the gloom into one of the little rooms near the coal bin. There, nourished by the smells of coal dust, dank earth, and what I identified years later as recent birth, I visited the new kittens. One, most magic of all, was white with blue eyes. I wanted to take her home, but Mother said no. When I visited again, the kittens and the mother were gone. Grandmother said they all had new homes.

The very best place of all, and the one I could count on to be unpopulated, was the attic. If you wanted to be really secret, you could take the closed backstairs from the kitchen to the second floor and then open the door from the back hall. You were immediately at the attic staircase, so immediately that it was hard to manage the door and get your feet on the steps, which had a tricky turn. There was no railing, and when you wanted to come down again, if your hands were full, the safest way was to sit on the attic floor and plant your feet firmly on a step before descending.

The treasures in the attic were more than I ever discovered. What remained unseen and finally discarded in those trunks and boxes which I never opened? But the things I knew were part of a ritual, a re-encounter with the past which became familiar and expected as I opened the lids and breathed in the hot sawdusty smell of the air I stirred into motion. One trunk held Grandmother's wedding

dress. That was a disappointment. Instead of white satin with a train and a veil, it was a navy blue suit. I asked Grandmother why she hadn't had a *real* wedding gown, and she said they were leaving right away on their wedding trip, and she thought a suit was more sensible. I thought it too bad to be sensible at one's wedding. There was a little-girl dress of Mother's, puff-sleeved and square-collared, made of heavy cream-colored silk with small yellow flowers. I was allowed to dress up in that.

Uncle Graham's rocking horse was in the attic until my father repainted it brown and saddled it in red velvet with blue reins. Then we took it home to live in my playroom for a while. I had to give it back when my cousin Graham grew old enough to ride it. It was a good rocking horse.

Best of all, in one of the little rooms under the eaves with its half-circle window crammed against the floor were Mother's dolls and the doll bed. There were three dolls with china heads and kid bodies that hemorrhaged sawdust. They had eyes that opened and closed and sometimes stuck. They had hair that had to be combed very carefully, or it would come out. Two had brown hair, but the beauty of the lot was blond and blue-eyed and named Ellen for Grandmother, who had been blond and blue-eyed. And *I* was named Ellen, and *I* was blond and blue-eyed, to Grandmother's gratification. The dolls' shoes were tan leather and laced above the ankles. There was a pair of blue mittens on a pink ribbon so they wouldn't be lost. There was a pink "wrapper" of warm blankety material. There was a wine-red dress with leg-o'-mutton sleeves and a sailor collar decorated with black braid. There were petticoats and unfamiliar underbodices and fine white dresses tucked and embroidered by Grandmother. The dolls and their clothes came downstairs and shared the Blue Bedroom with me until it was time for me to pack them away again.

As I trudged up the attic stairs and tenderly laid the dolls in their trunks, I knew this was only a temporary goodbye, until next time. The past was packed away for the moment, but it was resting, alive and waiting for me whenever I would look for it. The goodbyes were a little sad, but I was sure I would come back.

II

Meeting

It wasn't that I planned to do anything wrong. I didn't really plan at all. Only maybe I was starting to plan all along, from the time I learned about it.

It was just that it all seemed so strange. To have two grandmothers living in the same town and never to see one of them slowly became a puzzle.

Visits to my Grandmother Henley's house meant knowing about when-my-mother-was-a-little-girl. I slept in Mother's old room, the Blue Bedroom at the front of the house. I played in the garden where she had played and helped Grandmother pick the flowers planted long ago. I ate mulberries from the mulberry tree under which Grandmother, as a little girl, and later Mother had held their doll tea parties. I read over and over again the only two books which seemed to have survived my mother's and uncle's childhood. They were kept in a small bookcase in the upstairs hall, protected by a flowered curtain which slid on a rod. One was the first—the original—Oz book, which had been published when my mother was a child. Familiar though it was, I never tired of it. The other had belonged to my uncle. It was called *The Monkey Who Would Not Kill*, and I didn't really like it very much. It was all about a mischievous monkey whom many people wished to destroy but who always outwitted his attackers. He was really the monkey who would not *be* killed. I thought him unappealing because his mischief was usually a little hurtful. But remembering how my uncle had chased my mother with a tomahawk, I supposed he and the monkey must have had something in common.

But who could take me into my father's childhood? Who could tell me about his father, who died at forty-eight? Only my father told me those things, and he had been no more than ten at his father's death. Dud, who was older, would remember more. So would my grandmother.

There had been a Mexican hairless dog named Mex, a member of the family before my father was born. Mex was the only dog that ever disliked my father, and he snapped at his lisle stockings, nipping his legs as my father slid down the banisters. Dud would know about that. She would have known Mex when *he* was the baby of the family.

I had no idea where I would go when I started out for a walk that summer afternoon. One lovely thing about visits to Atchison was the freedom to explore, the sense of safeness, of being surrounded by friends wherever I went.

"You're Mrs. Henley's granddaughter, aren't you?" the woman at the candy store said, allowing me to fish around in the candy bowl for the prize which I most liked instead of grabbing blind.

Peacefully, I strolled under the elms shading the sidewalk from the summer sun. Beyond the candy store, past the Jones' house where my friend, Amy Jones, lived. I was on Fourth Street.

And then I was at the corner. Across the street two houses down, I could see the front porch of the house where my grandmother and my aunt lived. Maybe one of them might be sitting on the porch, and I could say hello. And then I could say who I was, and they would be so glad! Then everything would be all right, everyone would be happy, and they would all say I had done it.

Grandmothers, I knew, were always glad to see you. I didn't have an aunt, not really, but when my uncle Graham married Aunt Mavis, she had asked me to be the flower girl. After the ceremony, which was held at home, I announced that I was hungry. Aunt Mavis in her wedding gown took me into the pantry and cut me a piece of what I fondly believed was *the* wedding cake, though I realized later that it was probably a spare. I devoured it and announced, "I'm still hungry," to which my mother said firmly, "No, you're not," and turned down Aunt Mavis's offer to cut another slice.

A *real* aunt would probably be even nicer.

I was in front of the steps leading from the sidewalk to the porch. Two rocking chairs were on the porch, but no one was in them . . .

I paused, and then I mounted the steps.

I rang the bell and waited. Beyond the curtained front door, the house seemed to come alert and then to wait, too. I had the feeling of being seen. Then a figure moved behind the door, and a finger pushed the starched gauzy curtain an inch aside. One dark eye looked out.

The door opened. A large dark-haired woman stood there.

This was my aunt.

The woman smiled—slightly, but she smiled. Mother had said that Dud liked children.

I had several speeches ready, but they didn't come. I just looked at her. After a moment she said, as if to cue me in my lines, "If you're selling for the Girl Scouts, we can't buy anything, but if you'll wait a minute, I'll bring you a cookie."

"Are you Miss Paulsen?" I said. That sounded strange. I had never used that last name for anyone but my parents or me.

"Yes." She still must have thought I had her on some list.

"Hello-Aunt-Dud-I'm-your-niece," I said in a rush. She went rigid, her hand still on the doorknob. "I'm Ellen. Paulsen," I added.

I sensed another figure behind her in the dim hall.

"Who is it, Dud?" said a heavier voice.

Dud half turned from the door, still holding the knob.

"She says she's Frederick's—" she said over her shoulder.

Another silence. Then, "Let her come in," said the far voice.

"I don't think that's wise," Dud began, but my grandmother—my grandmother!—came closer to the door. I could see her then, tall, dark graying hair, eyes with my father's shadows under them. "Come in," she said to me.

Dud reluctantly opened the door another few inches, and I stepped into the hall.

"Come sit down," said my grandmother, and we all three went through the archway into the living room. The room was dim. The blinds were all drawn. The furniture was massive and upholstered in heavy, dark material. The woodwork was dark and shiny. Everything appeared to be tan or brown.

I chose a deep stuffed chair that seemed to swallow me. Dud and my grandmother sat opposite me, Dud in a straight-backed dining room chair. They were both very erect. My father always told me to stand up straight and deplored my mother's tendency toward round shoulders.

They looked at me. Dud spoke.

"That's Papa's chair she's sitting in."

I must have looked puzzled, for my grandmother said, "Your grandfather's."

"Oh." My grandfather had died when my father was the age I was now. I liked my grandfather. My father had told me how he played with his children, how he carried a flaming Christmas tree to a window and dropped it in the snow, how he took care of

The Other Grandmother

things. I settled back into the comforting arms of his chair. Grand-fathers protected you.

Still the two pairs of eyes looking at me.

Then, "She has Papa's coloring," said my grandmother. I had always thought that I was blond and blue-eyed like my mother's mother.

Now that I was here, I had nothing to say.

"You are a beautiful child," said my grandmother after another silence.

Dud seemed to rouse. "Don't let that go to your head," she said.

"Are you smart in school?" asked my grandmother.

"I guess so," I said. "I've had two double promotions."

"There are better things than being smart," said Dud. Then, "Your father didn't start school until he was nearly eight, and he wasn't sixteen when he entered the university."

"I know," I said. Did that sound too smart?

"How do you know?"

"He told me."

"He would."

I shrank farther back into my grandfather's chair.

"Those Henleys sent her," Dud turned to her mother. "To spy. Didn't they?" Back to me.

"No. Nobody sent me. I just came."

"Doesn't anybody know you're here?"

"No. I was taking a walk—and I just decided—" Now I was afraid that I seemed sneaky or disobedient.

Dud gave a snort and folded her arms.

My grandmother was absorbing me with her eyes. She had the kind of look I had caught on my father's face sometimes when he came to see me in school entertainments, a look of concentration that saw no one else. After another silence she said gently, "Would you like a cookie?"

"There aren't any left," said Dud and then, "She'd better go, Mama. It's time for your nap."

"I'm not tired," said my grandmother.

"You'd better go," said Dud rising. "You've seen us. You can make your report."

I struggled out of the depths of my grandfather's chair, my fingers lingering for a moment on the bas relief of the dusky cut velvet.

Dud stood until she saw that I was coming, then preceded me to the door. She held it sternly open as I entered the hall. Behind me I heard the rustle of my grandmother's dress.

We all stood at the door. I half turned. Weren't you supposed to kiss your grandmother good-bye? This grandmother stood apart from me, her hands folded in front of her. Dud was waiting.

Dancing school manners came to my rescue. "I'm very glad to have met you," I said.

Dud opened the door wider. I stepped onto the porch.

Then Dud made the response which I had been taught one gave. Only she changed it.

"Don't come again," she said.

I thought I heard my grandmother say, "Good-bye," as Dud closed the door.

My father came to drive us home. We planned to stay overnight in Columbia, Missouri, even though it was still summer, and the Tigers wouldn't be playing football.

On the way we picked up two college boys who were hitch-hiking back to school. My mother invited them to share the picnic lunch my grandmother had had the maid pack in a wicker basket: cold fried chicken, thin bread-and-butter sandwiches, a thermos of minted lemonade, and a chocolate cake with chocolate icing. My mother talked for a long time about how polite those boys were, and how, when they went to sleep in the back seat, they stuck their feet out the windows of our open Jewett touring car so they wouldn't scratch our luggage.

After dinner in Columbia my father said we would walk over to the university campus and look at the columns. My father wore a small gold column pinned to his watch fob, symbol of his alma mater. He told me how the six columns were all that remained after a long ago fire and sang me the song that ended,

"And may they be ever so standing
When Kansas is under the sod."

That was a song to be sung at the bonfire rallies before the Kansas-Mizzou football game, a game which my father and my uncle, a K.U. graduate, replayed all year until the next game.

My mother was tired, so only my father and I strolled over to the university. After the song, after we viewed the columns, we left the campus, walking through the summer dusk past quiet houses where porch swings and rockers creaked in the shadows, where only a few kitchen lights glowed as the last dinner dishes were washed.

Suddenly my father said, "I used to live down that street when I was in college."

"You did? There?"

"Yes. With my mother and Dud."

"Which house?"

"The one with the white porch. That's where I lived when the cocker spaniel followed me home."

Ordinarily I would have begged for that story again and wanted to look at the porch. The little dog had followed my father home and waited patiently for him to come out again. No matter how many times my father returned him, the dog persisted in coming back, until finally the owners gave him to my father.

But tonight I didn't want to see another house where Dud and my grandmother had lived. I didn't say anything.

I could feel my father looking at me as we walked along the quiet street. Finally he said, "One time when I was a boy I went to a bakery with my father."

I relaxed, holding his hand. A story about my grandfather would be safe.

"He loved to buy things, and he was walking around the bakery saying, 'I'll take a dozen of those—and give me a dozen of these.' A little boy about my age was watching outside the window. Finally he motioned to me, and when I went to the door, he whispered, 'Could you get me one of *those?*' It never occurred to me that I couldn't, so I went and got him a handful of cookies, just the way my father did things.

"But then after we left the bakery, I began to think. I hadn't told my father what I had done, so maybe I had been stealing. And I didn't know what to do. I thought I had done something wrong, though I hadn't meant to.

"So finally I got up my courage and told my father. He was swinging along, still feeling fine the way he always did after he'd bought something. And he said, 'Oh, that's all right. The girl counted those in.' But then he saw I had been worried, and he said, 'Always tell me when something bothers you. Don't try to keep it to yourself. Because maybe it really isn't as bad as you think.' "

We walked on in silence for a few more paces. I was still holding his hand. Then he said, "Something's bothering you, isn't it?"

"Daddy," I blurted, "I didn't mean to do anything wrong! I just wanted—to talk about when you were a little boy."

And then I told him. His hand tightened on mine, but we kept on walking.

"Daddy," I said at the end, "I'm sorry." I didn't know why, exactly, but feeling myself miserable again outside that closed door, I felt very sorry.

"You didn't do anything wrong," said my father in a tight voice. We had reached our hotel now, and the lights from the lobby streamed out on us. I could see my father's face, and he looked angry and sad all at once with the shadows dark under his eyes. "You didn't do anything wrong. It's my fault. I should have protected you." He broke off and pulled me back from the entrance.

"Tell me—" he didn't seem to know what to say next. "—Did you talk about what you do in school?"

"I told them I'd had two double promotions. I know that sounds like bragging, Daddy, but they—she—your—mother—asked me if I was good in school."

"That's all right. What else did she say? Did she say anything—nice—to you?"

I thought. It had been such a strange, dim room. Everything had been so different from what I had expected that I almost couldn't remember what had happened.

"She said I had your father's coloring. She said—" this was hard to repeat—"she said I was a beautiful child."

My father straightened and let out a sigh. The hand holding mine seemed to relax, to hold me in a warmer clasp.

"Let's go in and find Mother," he said.

After I had been put to bed in the room adjoining theirs, the door cracked open so I'd know where they were, I could hear the murmur of their voices. Once my father's rose, "—to do to a *child*!" he said in a sort of wail.

But whatever they were saying to each other, it was all right now. I had told, and it was all right. I could forget it had ever happened. Still hearing the murmur, I went to sleep.

∴   ∴   ∴

·:·

But that wasn't the way things should be.

From the books I read, *Little Lord Fauntleroy*, *The Little Colonel*, and others, I knew that children *always* could heal family estrangements, could make themselves treasured and beloved by the most implacable adults.

Many nights as I lay in bed waiting for sleep—and after sleep came—I comforted myself with a different story.

·:·

12

"Sing Mir Dein Lied"

If I could just make it to the corner without looking, I'd be all right. If I passed that spot, I could finish my walk from Sunday School. I concentrated on seeing myself at the dinner table at Grandmother's house, safely surrounded by the family. Grandfather would stand to carve the roast while Grandmother surveyed the table with mild approval. Noon sunlight would be streaming in the windows now. Now. If I just didn't look across the street. . .

I looked.

A figure was standing on the porch. It was my grandmother. She stood there, very tall and still, wearing something long and dark, and she was watching me. She raised her arm and beckoned to me.

A deliciously uncomfortable thrill of fear and fascination shot through my stomach. Remembering to look both ways before crossing the street, I crossed Fourth Street and stood at the bottom of the terrace, looking up at her.

"Ellen," she said formally, "if you're out for a walk some day and want to rest a while, you may stop here for a few minutes."

I think I said, "Oh," but maybe I only stared at her dumbly.

She turned to re-enter the house.

"Come by the back gate," she said. "Through the alley." Then she went in and closed the front door.

∴   ∴   ∴

At the Fourth Street corner before my other grandmother's house, I turned up the side street and walking the depth of one lot I found the alley. I hadn't even known it was there, sliced between two high terraces. The surface was uneven and scattered with cinders. A high hedge along the alley edged the boundaries of my grandmother's backyard.

The gate was of wooden slats which cut off the view of the yard. I found the latch, looked quickly down the alley to be sure no one saw me—that seemed essential—and slipped inside.

It was really a fairly pedestrian backyard. Unlike my Grandmother Henley's, this was a place without flowers. The grass was neatly trimmed, edging the walk from the gate to a back porch. The only sign that the place was inhabited was a rope clothes line strung between two trees. One white dish towel flapped in the breeze.

I climbed the porch steps and looked for a bell. There didn't seem to *be one, so I rapped on the wood of the door. Almost immediately, the door opened. My grandmother stood there. "Come in, Ellen," she said.*

In all of our time together, my grandmother was formal and unbending. Dud, wary and watchful, was at the edge of the scene, never quite of it but always there. My grandmother never touched me. Once we sat together on the couch while she handed me photographs from a cardboard box which she held in her lap. There were several of my father as a wispy-looking baby whom I secretly didn't think was very cute. And there was one taken when he was about my age, a big-eyed little boy whom I could recognize neither as my father nor as someone I could know and play with as a contemporary.

My grandmother would bring me lemonade and something to eat, macaroons or once a crisp, cinnamon-tasting cookie sprinkled with sugar. Dud would watch me as if she were afraid I would take too many cookies. Once I heard her in the kitchen say to my grandmother, "Those Henleys would be so mad if they knew."

"That's not why we're letting her come."

"That's why I'm letting her come."

"You're to tell no one," my grandmother said in a fierce whisper. "No one. They'd stop her." She was frowning when she came back into the living room with a plate of cookies.

"Does your father still speak German?" she asked me once.

"No—well, sometimes a little. Sometimes he sings me songs."

"What songs?"

"I don't know. One that goes 'Do, do—' "

"Du, du liegst mir im Herzen," said my grandmother quickly. She sang the line in a low, full voice. "Is that it?"

"Yes," I said, memories of being much younger, rocked on my father's lap while he sang to me, suddenly coming back.

"Do you know the words?" she asked me. I shook my head. "Would you like to learn them?"

I would. So I had my first German lesson. She didn't praise me, but she was patient and clear, singing the phrases over and over and waiting for me to repeat. She sent Dud from the room when she began to correct me. And at last I knew it, all of it.

"So, so, wie ich dich liebe. So, so, liebst du auch mich," I sang absently as I colored a new paper doll dress. I was sitting on the floor before the fire in our library at home.

My father in his big chair in the alcove lowered his paper. "Where did you learn that?"

I stopped short. I hadn't realized what I had been singing. "That's 'Du, Du—' You sing it to me."

"I'd forgotten the second verse," he said. "Where did you learn it?"

"I don't know. I forget."

He looked at me strangely, started to say something, then stopped. "Lena didn't sing that, did she?" Lena was the maid we had had when I was a baby, whom we saw sometimes on our trips to Atchison. "The punkin," she still called me much to my embarrassment, though I liked Lena.

"I don't know. I guess."

I was careful after that.

"How do you say 'Merry Christmas' in German?" I asked my father.

" 'Fröliche Weihnachten'," he said. "Why?"

"I just wondered.—How do you spell it?"

He spelled it while I laboriously lettered it out. He came and stood over me as I wrote, showing me how to make the umlaut. "Why are you so interested?"

"I just wondered.—Is that what you said at Christmastime when you were a little boy?"

"Yes. When I was a very little boy. Before I went to school."

"To your father and mother and sister?"

"Yes. Why?"

"I just wondered."

The afternoon before we were to take the sleeper to Atchison, I worked alone in my room. Mother was busy with last-minute packing and the details of closing the house for several days, so I was relatively undisturbed.

"What are you doing, dear?" as she passed my door.

"Making Christmas cards."

"That's nice," she said absently, hurriedly, and didn't ask to see.

I had a dummy ready in case anyone approached. Otherwise, I worked on my main project: a heavy sheet of blue construction paper on which I had pasted many gummed gold and silver stars. In glue I had written FRÖLICHE WEIHNACHTEN and then sprinkled gilt dust over the sticky surface. I had a hard time making the gold adhere evenly, and I kept sticking more on. My nose and throat began to feel scratchy as I bent over my work. I coughed. I had to let the paper dry. The last thing before we went to the station, I carefully rolled the paper into a scroll, tied it with a gold ribbon, and tucked it into the small suitcase in which I carried the treasures that must accompany me.

I didn't sleep well in my Pullman berth. I felt restless and anticipatory, and I was either too hot or too cold. It seemed a long night, almost as long as Christmas Eve.

Grandfather and Grandmother awaited us at the depot, or rather at the railroad crossing by the mill office, which was where the Pullman car stopped. Grandfather, who had probably been there for at least half an hour, was pacing sternly up and down the siding, timing the train's arrival, his gold pocketwatch open in his hand. Grandmother, snug in furs in the back of the Hudson, bundled me beside her and tucked the black sealskin lap robe around me.

"Gracious! Your knees are bare!"

"All the girls wear high socks, Grandma."

The house smelled of Christmas and felt like Christmas. A wreath was on the door, and Grandmother had made the cookies cut into stars and Christmas tree shapes and decorated with red and green sugar, silver sprinkles, and red hots. But I had to go through my usual arrival routine for any season—playing the player piano in the front room and listening to the rosy-throated conch shell used as a door stop by the vestibule door and marveling at the iridescent blue-green seashell paired with it.

I dashed through the house, becoming reacquainted. "Calm down, calm down," laughed my mother. "You have several days to go to Christmas yet. You'll be worn out."

I went to the attic to bring down Mother's three china-headed dolls. I had to dress them for the holidays.

"Were you coughing?" asked my mother, pausing by my door on her way to dress for an afternoon "open house" which my parents and grandparents were to attend.

"A little. It's the dust in the attic."

"Why don't you take a little nap while Daddy and I are out? Or at least lie on your bed and read. Grandmother has charlotte russe for dessert. You want to be able to eat a good dinner so you can have it."

"Yum," I said, although just then I didn't feel very hungry.

Mother lingered for another moment. "I think maybe you've had too many cookies already. Don't eat any more."

"All right." I had my own plans.

"Oh, dear!" I heard my grandmother at the front door. "Look how it's snowing! Do you think we should go?"

"Of course we should go!" my father said grandly. "I'll get you there and back."

Their good-byes rang in the front hall for a moment after the door closed. I went to my bedroom window and watched the Hudson lumber away from the curb, my father at the wheel, my grandfather looking responsible next to him in the front seat, and my mother and grandmother swaddled under the fur robe in back.

I opened my small suitcase and took out the blue scroll. I tiptoed down the front steps, listened in the hall for the busy sounds in the kitchen, took my hat and coat from the many-branched clothes tree, eased open the heavy vestibule door, closed it quietly behind me as Nancy Drew would have done, opened the outer door and stepped into the cold, wet air on the front porch.

It was snowing heavily by now and blowing. I bent my head into the wind, but the cold stung into my face. I was tired before I reached the corner.

It seemed a very long way, much longer than in summer. Once I sat down on a curb, but the cold and damp seeped through my coat so I got up and went on. The entrance to the alley was white and unmarked by footprints or wheel tracks. I struggled with the gate latch which was frozen in place. I started to cry a little. Everything seemed so hard! Finally, it moved, and I pushed the gate open against the snow piling on the walk. There was a light in the kitchen. I pulled myself up the porch steps, slipping a little, my shoes soaked through. I felt as if my socks were wet, too.

"Why, Ellen!" Dud seemed shocked to see me shivering at the back door.

"Ellen!" My grandmother opened the door, pulling me in. "What are you doing out in this weather?"

"I wanted to—bring you this." I pulled the heavy blue paper, crumpled and wet, from under my coat. I handed it to my grandmother. "I made it." She barely looked at it. She was looking at me instead. "It says 'Merry Christmas' in German." I felt very tired, and my teeth were chattering.

"You're wet through," said my grandmother. "And your feet—how did you come here?"

"I walked," I said. "I wanted to bring you—" I suddenly began to shake.

My grandmother was unbuttoning my coat.

"We'll have to get you warm and dry. Let's get you to bed."

"Mama—" Dud began.

"In Frederick's old room," said my grandmother. "Dud, bring me one of my flannel nightgowns." She was leading me up the stairs. They seemed very long and steep. I could hardly lift my feet.

"Mama—" said Dud again.

We were in the bedroom now. My grandmother seated me on the bed and was taking off my shoes. My teeth wouldn't stop chattering.

"I want a hot water bottle, Dud," she said as Dud came into the room with the nightgown. It kept falling off my shoulders, but my grandmother tightened the drawstring at the neck and turned back the sleeves. Then she pulled down the covers and helped me into bed. "I think we'd better fix her a hot toddy, too."

"Mama!" It was almost a wail. "She can't *stay here!"*

"She can't do anything else," said my grandmother. "The child's burning up with fever."

I didn't feel burning up. I couldn't get warm.

Dud came back with the hot water bottle and a cup. My grandmother wrapped the hot water bottle in a towel and tucked it at my feet. Then she began feeding me the toddy. I was promptly sick, all over the blanket.

"Oh, dear!*" said Dud.*

"It's all right," said my grandmother. "Get another blanket. And a damp cloth." She pulled the foul-smelling blanket off the bed, pushed it at Dud, and sitting on the side of the bed began to sponge my face and hands with the cloth Dud brought.

I lay back. Huddled under the covers, I fell asleep.

When I awoke, my mother and father and Dr. Charley were all there. Dr. Charley was saying, "Now, let's get this under your tongue, Ellen," and then he held my wrist. His fingers were cool.

"Probably flu," he said as he frowned at the thermometer.

"Oh, no!" my mother moaned.

"It hasn't been as bad as it was after the war," said Dr. Charley. "Still, her fever's pretty high."

"We'll take her right back to Mother's," said my mother, but Dr. Charley said, "Not in this weather, Elizabeth. She'd better stay right here."

In a low voice, he said to my father, "—danger of pneumonia."

My mother looked wildly around. Dud and my grandmother stood at the bedroom door.

"She's my child. I want to take care—"

"We haven't room for you here, Elizabeth," said Dud.

"I can take care of her," said my grandmother.

"I can't just leave her—" said my mother. I wished they'd all go away.

"I'll stay," said my father. "I'll sleep on the couch."

"You never fit on it," said Dud. "You're too long."

"She needs me!" my mother said.

"She can stay here," said my grandmother. She was looking at me.

"We can't settle this now," said my father. Vaguely, I understood that he was talking about more than today. "I'll stay with her. Mama is a good nurse."

It was dark when I woke again. Someone was sitting in the rocking chair next to my bed.

"My head hurts," I whimpered.

"I have a cool cloth right here." It was my grandmother. She bathed my face and then folded the cloth across my forehead. Then she took my hand, and rocking gently sang,

> *"Sing mir dein Lied*
> *Im Dämmerschein,*
> *Gieb mir Vergessen aller Pein—"*

The hall door creaked open and a dim light fell across my bed. My father was there, too.

"*Is she worse, Mama?*"
"*Shh! No. She'll go back to sleep—*

> *Nichts ist geblieben,*
> *Nacht ist so lang.*
> *Lass mir dein Lieben*
> *Und deinen Sang—*"

I did go back to sleep.

∴   ∴   ∴

Even in my imagination I couldn't bring off a happy ending.

The tightness in my mother's face when she mentioned Dud and my Other Grandmother blocked the possibility of any reconciliation, even one I might invent.

Somehow, though, I needed my Other Grandmother. It was as if I were a puzzle which I was slowing putting together, and my Other Grandmother held a key piece.

So for a long time I kept pretending.

Finally I stopped.

13

Impress

The *Atchison Daily World* was delivered every day by a boy on a bicycle. He paused at the curb and hurled the folded paper onto the porch. If Grandfather was there, he said, "Thank you, Tom," as he stooped for the paper, and Tom said, "You're welcome, Mr. Henley."

I didn't read the *World* much. It didn't have the funnies which I found in the daily Kansas City *Star* or the *Times*. One had "Winnie Winkle (The Breadwinner)" who was often almost losing her job but who had new clothes every day. And one had Ella Cinders, a spunky girl who continually outwitted a mean stepmother and two stepsisters. And there was "Dumb Dora," a chic flapper who seemed stupid but managed to run things so that in every last frame someone said, "*She's not so dumb!*"

The grown-ups read the *World*, though. It told what was happening in town and even in nearby places like Effingham.

The two people who decided if your name went in the *World* were Horace Henry and Nettie Belknap. Nettie Belknap said that her last name was spelled two different ways by the people who bore it. She said if you spelled it with a *k*, that indicated you were descended from royalty. Queen Elizabeth, she said. The relationship was proven because many of the Belknaps had red hair, and so did Queen Elizabeth. (Grandmother said Nettie used a henna rinse on hers.) There were some Belknaps who lived out on the edge of town and raised chickens. Nettie didn't associate with them. She said she always suspected they had added the *k*.

Nettie wore suits and flowered hats. The suits showed that she was a career woman. The flowered hats made her appropriately dressed for her job. Nettie was the Society Editor of the *Atchison Daily World*. It said so on the masthead, right under "Horace Henry, Editor."

My uncle Graham said that wasn't the only place Nettie Belknap was under Horace Henry, Editor. My mother said, "Graham! You're terrible!" Then she looked around the downstairs hall where they were standing in Grandmother's house and said, "Really?"

When important social events occurred in Atchison, Nettie Belknap either telephoned or appeared. Afterwards, she wrote them up for the society column. When the notices appeared in the *World*, you knew those parties had been important. During the summer visits that my mother and I made to Atchison there were many parties. Mother's friends gave luncheons for her, and Mother and Grandmother entertained. Grandmother would have long conversations at the wall telephone in the upstairs hall, describing the proposed party menu and the color scheme for the bridge tables set up in the library and living room.

"That was Nettie Belknap," Grandmother would say on hanging up. "She can certainly talk a long time." Both Grandmother and Mother always seemed a little scornful. But we always read Nettie's articles. The ones on Grandmother's and Mother's activities headed her columns and were very long.

I didn't know Horace Henry, but I knew he was famous. People in Atchison said so. He had written a book about a newspaper editor in a small town. Everyone said the town was Atchison. But people outside of Atchison knew about the book, too, and even now, some forty years later, you might run across someone who would say, "Oh, yes," if you mentioned Horace Henry and his novel. My father, who collected first editions, once found a few lines about the novel in a book collectors' magazine, so that proved that Horace Henry was famous.

Atchison people were proud of Horace Henry's fame, though sometimes surprised, when they traveled, to encounter people who didn't know about it. But it was satisfying, once one had established Horace Henry and his fame with an outsider, to be able to look wise and say, "Of course, in Atchison, we know about Horace Henry."

Horace Henry was a terrible man. Grandmother said that Mrs. Henry was afraid of her husband, that she never went anywhere and had had a nervous breakdown because of him. Their daughter, Cecile, was a friend of Mother's. During their girlhood sometimes Cecile spent the night with Mother after a dance because Horace Henry locked her out of the house. People said that Cecile left Atchison because her father was so mean to her.

But Cecile showed him. She wrote a novel too. And hers won a prize. One of the women's magazines, *Pictorial Review*, was it? or *Delineator*?, sponsored a contest for a novel to be published in its pages, and Cecile won. So she was famous right now, not a long time ago. We saw her story printed in a magazine that actually came to our house. Usually I was allowed to have the issues when Mother was through with them so that I could cut out the colored pictures of up-to-date mauve and green bathrooms and paste them in the old telephone book which I used as a paperdoll house. But Mother kept the two copies that contained Cecile's "serial." She could show people that she had a famous friend.

I never read the novel. It wasn't interesting to me, except to prove that Cecile was famous. But Atchison people looked wise and indicated with satisfaction that there was something unpleasant in it. What's more, they stated that it was really *true*, and that served Horace Henry right. Now the gullible world which had accorded him his fame would really *know*. At the time, I had no idea that first novels are often both autobiographical and therapeutic. The whole story struck me as marvelously unique.

When I was about fourteen, Mother and I were in town for a social event to which Nettie Belknap accorded lavish attention. Betty Ann Blake was being married. Betty Ann was the daughter of Mother's friends, Aunt Mildred and Uncle Cyrus. Uncle Cyrus managed the grain elevator which was part of the Graham Milling Company of which my uncle Graham was now president. Aunt Mildred came to or gave those luncheons that Nettie Belknap wrote about.

Aunt Mildred and Uncle Cyrus, looked remarkably alike, dark-haired, round-faced, and smiling, so their children, Jack and Betty Ann, looked alike too. Betty Ann was pretty, and Jack was handsome. Aunt Mildred and Uncle Cyrus were grown-ups, so I really didn't think about whether or not they were attractive.

Betty Ann was an older girl, to be admired, usually from a distance. But Jack was a hero. Everyone in town knew Jack Blake. He was a star high school athlete. And in the summer he played baseball. Sometimes I was in town and went to the games. Once, he needed a ride to a game, and Grandfather agreed to pick him up. Jack, neat and shining in his white uniform, was waiting on the curb when Grandfather and I pulled up in the Hudson. He was wearing his baseball cap and already had his glove on. He looked official, and I thought that we would look official, having him in our car.

"Hello, Mr. Henley. Hello, Ellen." I hadn't been sure he would remember my name, but he grinned and pulled the back door open and got in beside me, even though there was space up front with Grandfather. He even said, "How are you?"

Grandfather liked Jack. Everybody did. Grandfather was asking him whether we were going to win, and Jack said, "Gee, I sure hope so, Mr. Henley," and Grandfather chuckled and said, "You going to hit another homer for us like you did last time?" And Jack said, "Gee, I don't know. That was kind of lucky," and looked at me and shrugged a little, inviting me to understand. I found myself nodding. If I had been with one of the older high school boys at home, a star like that, I would have felt self-conscious and not known what to say. With Jack, it didn't matter whether I said anything. He made things seem easy between us, as if we were friends.

I don't remember if Jack hit another homer that night, but I do remember he was heroic. Everyone cheered whenever he came up to bat. He didn't pay any attention to the cheers. He looked very strong and determined, and he stared the pitcher in the eye. And when he hit the ball with a terrific *crack*, I was screaming, "Come on, Jack!" just like everyone around me. When he wasn't doing something heroic himself, Jack was encouraging his teammates, cheering them on or consoling them when thing went wrong.

"Tough break," I heard him say when one struck out. "Next time!"

When the game was over, he came to where Grandfather and I were sitting and said, "Thanks for bringing me, Mr. Henley. I'm going with the team now." Then he looked at me and said, "Good night, Ellen," so anybody looking knew I knew him.

Mother and Grandmother considered Betty Ann's wedding worthy of notice. It was so important that Mother had brought with us my first long dress, so that I might wear it at the wedding. I had worn it before at some of the boy-girl parties which were an outgrowth of the dancing school classes at home. Mother had reluctantly allowed me to have it after I had suffered the humiliation of being the *only* girl in a short dress at one of those parties. My shame was only partly offset by the fact that the boy who had accompanied me (driven to the dance, as we were, by our fathers) was the only boy there in knickers. For the next party, he had long pants and I had my long dress, but we didn't go together.

The dress was a pale blue embroidered organdy with a deep ruffle on the bottom of the skirt and a taffeta sash. I suppose it wasn't really very different in style from the kind of dress I had worn for years to birthday parties, but I felt grown-up because it was long. Once she had capitulated, Mother liked it, too. She wanted me to wear it to Betty Ann's wedding, although her friends' children still wore short dresses. Mother said that things were a little behind in a small town, and that her friends would just have to realize that it was different in St. Louis.

I stood before the long mirror in the bedroom that had been my mother's when she was growing up. While she tied my sash, Mother told me about Aunt Mildred's wedding to Uncle Cyrus. Mother said Aunt Mildred's mother had been a very difficult, demanding woman, and it was hard to understand how Aunt Mildred turned out to be so pleasant. When Aunt Mildred got married, her mother insisted that Mildred help *her* dress, rather than the other way around. Adjusting my ruffle, Mother said that at this very moment Aunt Mildred was probably helping Betty Ann into her wedding dress, which was just how a mother should behave.

Betty Ann was being married at home. I knew the house, of course. Even though Betty Ann and Jack were older than I, I was often in their home when our parents met for family dinners and picnics. It was a rangy gray stucco house with open porches and French doors leading on to them. Always welcoming and comfortable, the house was dressed up for the wedding. Friends had stripped their gardens of white flowers, as years earlier they had contributed lilacs for Mother's wedding, and tall gladioli and madonna lilies stood in vases on the floor and on tables. Grandmother had contributed some of her tuberoses, and I recognized them in a bouquet mixed with babies' breath.

Under a bobbing millinery bouquet of her own, Nettie Belknap was flushed and beaming. The career-woman suit had given way to flowered chiffon, but her note pad and pencil showed that she was officially on duty. She darted through the crowd, laughing and chatting, making not very surreptitious notes. The women became more animated as she approached.

Horace Henry was there too. I had never seen him before. He was quite evidently willing to be seen. He had white hair and wore a black string tie, which nobody (except someone playing a country editor's role) wore any more. He had decided to become a character. He had also decided to become charming. "Elizabeth Henley's daughter?" he said when we were introduced. "I knew your mother when she was a young lady like you."

I thought he wanted to impress me because he thought *I* thought he was famous. So I was deliberately unimpressed. After all, I really was a young lady—almost—and anyway, I knew about Horace Henry, even if he didn't know I knew. He was a terrible man.

I also decided to be unimpressed with Sarah Margaret, Grandmother's niece. Sarah Margaret was my first cousin once removed. It was said that she and Jean Harlow had been friends when they were growing up, and that Sarah Margaret knew that Jean Harlow hadn't wanted to leave Kansas City to go into the movies. Her mother had made her. Sarah Margaret was now living in New York and was just visiting. So was I—just visiting. Sarah Margaret was wearing a silver dress and black nail polish. She smoked cigarettes through a long holder and looked you in the eye and didn't seem glad to see you. I was surprised that she was so small. She had been a big girl when we ran around Great-grandmother's house that summer. Then I realized that all of the Grahams grew up small, and that Sarah Margaret was now grown up. She was quite pretty, but I decided that the black nail polish was to prove she was from New York and to impress the locals. It was rather in the category of Horace Henry's string tie. Since I wasn't a local, was, in fact, from St. Louis, I decided not to be impressed.

Betty Ann was Sarah Margaret's age, and she had also been involved in those activities at Great-grandmother's house. They probably took place after Great-grandmother's death when Uncle Wesley, Grandmother's brother and Sarah Margaret's father, lived there after his divorce. It was with Betty Ann that I saw the ghost.

We had been playing in the yard of Great-grandmother's house when Betty Ann decided that we should wash our hands in the downstairs lavatory. I stood aside as she opened the lavatory door. And there, absolutely motionless, with its hands held in front of it, stood—a white ghost! We froze for a terrible moment and then, screaming, ran all the way up to the third floor where Sarah Margaret was having a decorous chat with the housekeeper. I can see them now as we burst into the room. They turned their heads, politely tolerant but slightly annoyed at the interruption. We panted out our news, and Sarah Margaret said scornfully that there was no such thing as ghosts, and that she would prove it. She led the way righteously downstairs. Bravely she opened the lavatory door while we hung back.

The floor was littered with clean white huck towels.

"See," said Sarah Margaret, the personification of the rational mind, "nothing but towels." And she held some up for us to see.

Betty Ann was a beautiful bride, and Jack was wearing a white coat. He was the usher and found seats on the folding chairs, pristine with their white covers, for the older guests. The rest of us stood. I leaned against the archway between the hall and living room, where I could get a good view of the staircase.

Then one of Aunt Mildred's friends started to play the wedding march on the piano in the front hall. The groom and his best man, looking a little sheepish, entered the living room from the dining room. They had come down the back stairs and had been waiting in the kitchen. Jack, looking as stern as when he faced the opposing pitcher, stepped up to stand at attention behind them. Betty Ann's maid of honor had been hiding in the kitchen, too, and she came through the front hall, doing the hesitation step that you were supposed to do going down the aisle in a church wedding.

And finally, Uncle Cyrus and Betty Ann descended the staircase. Uncle Cyrus was crowded against the wall, turned a little sideways, so that Betty Ann would be on the railing side where she could be seen. They looked both serious and smiling. But then they began to jostle each other as they came down the narrow staircase, and for a minute they both laughed a little. They stopped laughing when they came to the bottom. They paused to get even with each other, looked down at their feet so that they could each start off with the same one, and then they did the hesitation step across the hall into the living room. They were right together.

The woman playing the piano couldn't see when Uncle Cyrus and Betty Ann got to the makeshift altar, so she kept on playing. Then Nettie Belknap gave a quick bob of her head that made all the flowers on her hat shake, and the pianist stopped.

The Presbyterian minister, who had preceded the other men into the living room and had been standing in a position of authority, facing the guests, for some time, cleared his throat and began the service. When he asked who gave this woman, Uncle Cyrus said he did. Then he stepped back and looked down at Betty Ann's train, seeming to wonder whether to step over it or to walk around it. Finally, he walked around and sat down next to Aunt Mildred in the folding chair saved for him.

I was surprised at how short the ceremony was. In no time at all, the minister said that Betty Ann and her husband were married. After all the preparation, I felt a little let down.

Betty Ann and her new husband embraced and turned to face the guests. They stood there, smiling and blinking a little. Betty Ann looked happy but somewhat uncertain, as if she were waiting for something to happen but wasn't sure what it was. There was no music to start them marching back to the hall to form the receiving line.

Then Jack in his white coat stepped out from behind the best man and with a stride was in front of Betty Ann. He took her by the shoulders and turned her toward him. She lifted her bride's face, all shining and hopeful, and he bent and kissed her. Then he seemed to give her shoulders a final squeeze, bobbed his head in a brief, reassuring nod, dropped his hand and stepped back from her.

And then a strange thing happened. Suddenly Jack's face grew very red and seemed to balloon up. He began to cry.

I had never seen a boy cry openly like that, not one Jack's age. But he just stood there, facing the room, crying. He didn't try to hide it. Finally he got out his handkerchief, mopped his face, laughed, and put his handkerchief away.

And *that* impressed me.

14

"Nichts ist Geblieben"

The Other Grandmother died. No one informed us. The phone rang when we were all at breakfast one morning, and my mother answered.

"Yes. Yes. Thank you. We appreciate your call."

My father, about to go to New York on business, looked quizzically at my mother as she returned to the table. "I'll tell you on the way to the train," she said.

That afternoon when I came home from school, Mother showed me the article in the morning paper. The friend who had called had seen it and was offering sympathy. The headline read: "Local Telephone Co. Executive's Mother Dies."

"Dud sent that in," said my mother. "She *wanted* him to find out that way. In the paper. She's that cruel." Then she looked at me. "You really don't remember her, do you?"

"Dud?"

"No. Your—Daddy's mother. You saw her just that one time."

I thought back to that dim room. It must have been two or three years before. In my life it seemed a long time. So much had happened for me, leaving grade school behind, entering junior high school. So I said, "Not really. Not very well."

"Good." Mother seemed relieved.

But then one image sprang sharply before me: my grandmother, motionless, apart from me, watching me as I stepped out of her house and her life. I could see her in my mind, but I couldn't yet read her expression. I pulled my attention back to what Mother was saying.

"I told Daddy when I drove him to the depot." She paused, seemed uncertain, then compelled. "He cried," she said. "He cried and said, 'After all, she was my mother.'"

I was stunned. I couldn't imagine my father crying. Neither of us said anything. Then the clock with the Westminster chimes which my father wound every Sunday struck six o'clock. The maid, trained to be punctual even when my father wasn't home, announced dinner.

Mother and I went into the dining room, and she asked me what had happened at school that day.

When it was time to elect a foreign language in high school, I chose German.

My mother rather favored French. It seemed to her to be more "cultured." She had studied French at Miss Bennet's Boarding School at Irvinton-on-the-Hudson in New York State, where she had been taught how to place one's feet when seated so that one might rise gracefully, as one had to when Miss Bennet entered the room. She taught me to say "Ploo de low see voo play" when I wanted more water. She would them refill my glass from the beading silver pitcher at her right hand, and I would say "Mer-see," and be moderately proud of myself. But my father was pleased that I wanted to study German, and I don't recall any real objections from Mother.

Daddy had grown up speaking German before he spoke English. I always thought it somewhat humorous that my Danish grandfather had left Denmark to escape Bismarck's government and had married into a German-speaking family. My grandmother had been born in the United States, but her parents had not, and like many

Germans they had clung to the old ways and the old tongue at home.

Memories reached back to touch lives of unknown ancestors in the old country. My father's grandmother, widowed and living with her Paulsen son-in-law, told the story told her by *her* grandfather. As a small boy in Germany, he was taken once a year by his mother to a gathering of her family. His father was not allowed to accompany them. His mother had come from a noble family but had married a commoner. Her child, carrying some of the noble blood, though somewhat dilute, was acceptable at such a reunion, but his father was not. He could remember a night ride in a carriage, up a winding drive overhung with trees. The road led up a mountain, with a lighted castle at the top. . . .

Where was that mountain? Who was the family? Had they accepted their daughter gladly on those once-a-year visits? Had she felt apologetic or defiant, returning without her rejected husband, with a son who she must have hoped would impress them all? Was she nervous? Wistful? Hopeful that there would be some magic moment of reconciliation? I mourned that lighted castle, lost forever at the top of its dark drive.

My father told me that one time when he wanted to pick up some easy credits in a college summer session, he took a German course, knowing he wouldn't have to work. When called on to translate an English sentence into German on the board, he dashed off an idiomatic expression that the class hadn't studied. The instructor said, "Where did you learn that?" and my father replied, "Did you ever look at my last name?" It was really Danish, but Germanic enough to confound a teacher. The story served to prove to me again my father's superiority to all other beings, including those in authority.

∴   ∴   ∴

About the same time, I began to study voice. That was my father's idea. Because I had a low speaking voice, he was convinced that I would be a contralto. In vindication of his prediction, I certainly strained on the high notes. He produced as my teacher a woman who had been his classmate (in one of his many classes!) in Carrollton, who now lived in St. Louis and was, I later realized, probably close to genteel poverty, having a mysteriously ill and absent husband and a daughter in college. (Many years later, the daughter made headlines by marrying a vice president of the United States.) I suppose that beyond wanting me to study voice and wishing to help an old acquaintance now in unfortunate circumstances, my father was more than willing for that old acquaintance to see how far the saloon owner's son had come, maintaining a large house with servants for his family of three during the Depression, which others—including obviously my teacher—were feeling severely.

Soon after the voice lessons started, my father presented me with some sheet music. He had doggedly searched music shops in South St. Louis, where songs in the German language were sold. This was one of his favorites, he said. I might like to learn it.

I propped the music up on the square rosewood piano with the word *Chickering* above the keyboard. The piano had belonged to my great-grandmother Graham and had come from the third-floor ballroom in her house. I read the song title, "Sing Mir Dein Lied," and the English subtitle, "Sing Me To Sleep." I scanned the words, all the way through. The English was a version, not a translation. The English emphasized the feeling of a love song, but the German included emotions of desolation and loneliness. I began to pick the tune out on the piano and sing the German to myself:

"*Sing mir dein Lied im Dämmerschein,*
Gieb mir Vergessen aller Pein (Give me forgetfulness of all pain)
Lang ist der Tag, mein Herz so Schwer (The day is long, my heart is
so heavy)
Wollt dass mein Leid vorüber wär (Would that my suffering were
over)."

Something was tugging at my memory. I was sure I had never
heard the song before, yet it seemed to be urging me to remember
something. I worked on:

"*Nichts ist geblieben* (Nothing is left)
Nacht ist so lang (Night is so long)
Lass mir dein Lieben (Leave me your love)
Und deinen Sang (And your song)."

I played that part over again. And suddenly, as if a picture had
been flashed on a screen above the piano, I saw my Other Grandmother as I had last seen her. She stood immobile, her hands
clasped before her as I was ushered out of the door. Did she hold
her hands to keep from reaching out to me? She was still, but her
eyes followed me until the closed door came between us.

Nichts ist geblieben. She might just as well have said it out loud.
She knew that she would never see her only grandchild again.
Nothing was left.

15

Over

My father was nearly eleven the summer that his father died. I never knew the cause of that death. "Stomach trouble," I heard once, and "summer pneumonia." I have two pictures of my grandfather, one a posed family portrait with Dud, my grandmother, my father at about six and Uncle Henry and my grandmother's sister Adelia, Henry's first wife. My grandfather looks to be a robust Dane, his watch chain draped across a portly stomach. Even in the black-and-white photograph one can discern the high color in his cheeks. My father said that he used to tell a story which he said explained his ruddy complexion. As a boy at home in Denmark, he was setting off fireworks in a patriotic celebration when some failed to go off. Ever impatient and active, he went to examine them. Just as he bent over to look, the fireworks exploded, and blew him, he *said*, over a fence. He claimed that his face remained red from then on.

That first picture looks like the man I have heard about, the man who "loved to see people eat," who carried vats of soups and stews from the kitchen at home to his saloon, swinging the buckets as he crossed the parlor and spotting the carpet with what he spilled.

The second picture is a snapshot, taken outdoors on what must have been a warm day. My grandmother is there, and my father, older than in the first picture, his eyes shut against the sunlight. And my grandfather is there, with a cane in his hand. He isn't old—he was only forty-eight when he died—but he looks some-how diminished. He is smiling, but it is the patient smile of some-one who has endured long pain. Was this the summer of his death?

However obscure the cause, the story of the night before his death was clear. My father emphasized in telling it that his father was not a superstitious man, that he insisted that everything had a reason. Nor was my father superstitious. But he was aware of the old belief that a clock striking thirteen foretold a death in the house. My grandfather was ill with his mysterious fatal illness. My grandmother and one of her brothers were sitting up with him. He was to have medicine at midnight. They sat in silence in the darkened room, half dozing until the clock began to strike. Then they counted wordlessly. Ten—eleven—twelve—*thirteen!* The first sound either of them made came from my grandmother's brother, "*No, it didn't!*"

They rose and went into the hall. Downstairs the dining room clock, a few minutes slower, struck. They stood, counting. Again—ten—eleven—twelve—thirteen.

The next morning my grandfather died.

My father predicted that he himself would die at forty-eight as his father had. For much of my childhood, that age seemed im-possibly remote to me. Perhaps it did to my father also.

The summer after I turned eleven, when my father was in his early forties, he had what was called heat prostration. He had always been a strong and vigorous man, having overcome, partly by force of will, a sickly childhood. He was proud of his energy and en-durance. He believed that one could accomplish anything one wished if one set one's mind to it. He proudly claimed that he had never been drunk and never would be. He could control his physical reactions. But now he could not. Perhaps then the apprehension of his own mortality closed in on him.

It was a very hot summer, before homes were air-conditioned.

I don't remember much about the events, but the doctor said my father should take a three-month vacation from the office. We rented a cottage at a Michigan resort, I was allowed to take a friend along (as an only child, companionship for me wasn't automatic) and we went off for what seemed to me a pleasant vacation.

The resort was an active, self-contained summer colony. Many families from the St. Louis area vacationed there regularly. Their sojourns were long enough to sustain leisurely activities, including, for some, amateur theatricals with their many rehearsals. During my parents' courting days, my father had reveled in such performances, and now he took part again. The casts were all large, to give all would-be participants a part. Starring roles went to the young and comely who could sing and dance, but my father made his presence felt, at least to his own satisfaction.

It was through such activities and through his walks that my father extended his acquaintanceship. Ever an early riser, he took walks before breakfast and recounted—sometimes—his conversations en route as we met later at the breakfast table. There were some girls a little older than I who also came from St. Louis, though from another suburb, and they were often on their front porch as he went by. Another large St. Louis family had a complex of cottages. One was occupied by two unmarried sisters, probably then in their late twenties or early thirties, whom I identified only vaguely.

Once, home in St. Louis, my mother and I went to see my father in his office.

"I think one of those sisters who was in Michigan last summer was on the elevator with us," I said to my father.

"Well, did you speak to her?" he asked.

"No."

"Why not?"

"I wasn't sure."

I forgot all about the incident, but years later, when she had more to tell me, my mother reminded me of it. She also said that the young woman didn't get off the elevator when we did, although my father's office was one floor from the top story of the building which housed only the president's office and conference rooms.

Back home at the end of that summer there were some changes, of small significance to me. My parents bought some air conditioners, bulky noisy things that sat on the floor. They placed one in the dining room, the only room with doors that could close it off from the hall, and brought in two easy chairs and two reading lamps which they placed in the bay. The second unit was placed in their bedroom. Perhaps it was that fall that they substituted twin beds for the double bed they had had since the beginning of their marriage. My father said that my mother didn't lie quietly in bed. The new beds were placed on either side of the front window in their room. Often my father would fall asleep on the couch downstairs in the living room while my mother read or sewed in the adjoining library. I don't know when they went to bed, sometime after I did.

About that year, knitting became a popular pastime with young girls. Many of my friends learned to knit, some actually to become expert enough to make usable garments, but many, I suspected, mainly to have something to show. They carried their knitting bags and pulled out needles and balls of yarn whenever they could and were apt to say "*Shh!*" suddenly in the midst of a conversation and begin to count in a fierce, self-important whisper.

I wasn't interested in becoming a knitter. Sometimes, in fact usually, I resisted going along with the crowd unless they were doing something that I really wanted to do. I had nothing against the bonafide knitters, could, in fact, admire their finished products and the soft balls of colored yarn, but I had no wish to join them in their activity. I did sometimes consult with them over choices of patterns or colors.

A new knit shop opened on the main street of our suburb. It was run by the two sisters from the summer resort. My mother told me not to go in there if I was with other girls who did. I don't recall what reason she gave me; it was unlike her to offer no explanation. I think she said something about those young women not being "nice." It was years before she told me why.

Ours had always been an affectionate family. "My two!" my father would carol, wrapping his long arms around Mother and me both at once and holding us, while the dog went wild running around us and jumping in his effort to get into the magic circle. And sometimes Mother and I together would sit on his lap in the big chair in the library alcove.

Of course, as I grew older, demonstrations of that sort became fewer. I don't think that I even noticed any change. I did notice the irritation between my parents. It seemed to me that one or the other became angry over minor episodes, and dinner times were often strained with the tension between them. Why did they make so much out of so little? I wondered, trying to chew quietly so that I did not attract attention to myself.

Some evenings, I picked out tunes on the Chickering piano in the music room, and my father and I, neither of whom was musically accomplished, would sing them. Singing was part of our life together from my earliest days. I was told that my father used to rock me and sing, beating out the tempo on me until my mother would protest, "Don't hit her so *hard!*" and he would respond, "Oh, she loves it!"

I probably did. What he sang, of course I don't recall, but throughout my life certain songs have had an unaccountable familiarity. Old, old songs that I can't remember learning. Once in a while as I grew older, my father would say, "My mother and aunt used to sing that." Usually, though, the songs he sang, which no one else seemed to know, went unexplained.

Those weren't the songs we sang together at the piano. I had no music for them. We sang from a Missouri University song book ("Old Missouri, Fair Missouri," to the tune of a Cornell song which my father claimed Cornell "stole" from Missouri) or from my sheet music of current songs.

"I'll be faithful," we sang together one night, "Forever and ever, dear . . ."

My mother, on her way upstairs, called over her shoulder, "I don't like that song."

"Oh, then, we won't sing it," said my father, folding up the sheet music.

"It has too many memories," came my mother's voice.

My father said loudly, "Your memories are your own fault," and reopened the music.

Why did she have to add that last when he was being so nice about it? I wondered. One of them was always spoiling things.

One Mother's Day my father had planned a surprise. While Mother was at church he hung on the living room wall an oil painting which they had both admired. Then he sat down in the library with the Sunday paper and waited for her come home and make the discovery. When Mother came back, she was not in a good mood. Maybe she thought that my father had neglected to get her a Mother's Day present. Maybe there was some reason I didn't know. But she came in from putting the Buick in the garage, and she said something nasty to my father. He hit the floor with a roar, and, shouting something, he dashed into the living room and ripped the picture from the wall. I was terrified. I ran into the front hall and up the stairs. I stood in the upper hall looking into the stairwell. My father, the painting in one hand, strode into the hall, still shouting.

"Daddy! Oh, *please!*" I cried.

He didn't answer, but gave a kind of sob. Mother was saying something, sounding apologetic. I ran into my room and closed the door. I sat on the edge of my bed, breathing hard and staring at the door into my parents' empty bedroom. Then I got up and closed that door as silently as possible and sat on my bed again. The May breeze stirred the white dotted-swiss drapery of the canopy bed I had wanted. My parents had given me the grown-up bedroom furniture for Christmas, and my father had had it all set up in the music room before Christmas, sliding shut the heavy wooden door that usually was left hidden in the wall because it was cumbersome to move. Then after I had seen my Christmas surprise, the furniture was reassembled in my room, a dream room with pale blue wallpaper decorated with feathery sprays of pale yellow wheat. Grandmother had made a blue-and-yellow quilt and bolster cover for my bed. There were venetian blinds at the windows—I had wanted those, too—and blue-and-white Wedgewood fixtures for the curtain tiebacks. The curtains matched the canopy of the bed, and both bed and window draperies were held back with blue taffeta sashes lined with yellow. I had my small radio for listening to the "Hit Parade" and my own phone, a pale ivory one, on the bedside table. It was a perfect room. But I wasn't appreciating the perfection.

I continued to sit on the bed, not daring to turn on my radio or pick up a book, until there was a knock on my door.

Mother said that dinner was ready. So I went downstairs and sat in my usual place at the table and watched my father carve the Sunday roast.

∴   ∴   ∴

Dud lived on. She moved, we heard, and took a room in someone's home. The woman of the house would invite her to join the family for coffee and cake, but she never accepted. Sometimes she entered magazine contests ("Complete the Jingle") and sometimes she won a prize.

And sometimes she wrote other things. I didn't hear about them right away. But, home from college my sophomore year, I found myself my mother's unwilling confidante. Dud, she said, had written a postcard to my grandmother Henley. She said she knew my father was having an affair. How could she know what went on in other cities? Malevolence gets into the air and finds it target.

"Mama always said Elizabeth would drive Frederick to another woman," she wrote on the postcard my grandfather had sent to Mother. For no appropriate reason that I could see, it had a picture of the Atchison YMCA on the front. "I hope he breaks her heart."

My grandfather, true to his discipline of not berating another's actions, but fiercely protective of his wife, wrote to my father: "What you do is your own business, and I won't judge the truth of this accusation, but I don't think much of someone who would write this to Elizabeth's old and sick mother." To my mother, along with the postcard which was surely by then public knowledge, he sent a copy of his letter.

"Is it true?" I asked my mother. "Is he—having an—affair?" I was struggling for my recently acquired college sophistication. My mother pursed her lips. "How do you know?"

"A wife knows," said my mother, and suddenly I didn't want to know how she knew.

"Well," I said, striving to be practical, objective, "—are you going to get a divorce?"

"Ellen," said my mother, as if I were somehow at fault, "you know as well as I do that a divorced woman has no social standing."

∴   ∴   ∴

My father had always said that he would die at forty-eight, as his own father had. He was wrong. Actually, he was fifty-four.

Those last bewildering days in the hospital when the pain was so bad, he bit his lip and clenched his teeth and made no sound. But then, pushed over the edge by his pain and disintegration, the adult personality deserted him. My mother, there for the last hours, said that he called, "Mama!" and "Papa!" and, most heartbreaking of all, "—oh—*please!*" as if he had been taught that good little boys get what they want if they ask politely.

I was twenty-three with a child of my own, but my bewilderment was a child's bewilderment. My competent, reasoning father couldn't have been driven beyond the brink of control. He couldn't be *gone*.

I knew he had wanted cremation. An agnostic, he had said he wanted his ashes scattered from a plane—the romance of flying in World War I never left him—on the Missouri River. Mother chose to ignore his wishes. She had him packed into a box—he who fought claustrophobia in Pullman berths!—and shipped to Atchison to be buried in the cemetery there. But there wasn't room in the family plot, so new ground had to be broken in a lonely spot. (Years later, space became available, and Mother had him moved to join the Grahams and Henleys.)

There was only a graveside service. The young minister hadn't known him. He fell back on the Twenty-third Psalm.

"He's dead, he's really dead," I thought as, chilled by that January wind, I stared at the coffin.

Later, I wondered if I shouldn't have at least tried to carry out his wishes, but I had felt that they would upset Mother. But shouldn't I have asked for his favorite poem, that wild cry of independence from William Ernest Henley, the challenge of "Invictus":

> Out of the night that covers me,
> Black as the Pit from pole to pole,
> I thank whatever gods may be
> For my unconquerable soul.

I could see the flash of his teeth, the set of his jaw, as he declared triumphantly,

> "*I* am the master of my fate;
> *I* am the captain of my soul!"

"At least," said my mother afterwards, "it was a beautiful day." I had thought it was a raw, gray one.

A friend told my mother that she had called Dud to offer to take her to the funeral. Dud had thanked her but said she preferred to do her grieving alone. What grieving, I thought, what grieving?

Staying in my uncle's home after the funeral, I stood at a front window looking across Fifth Street. My uncle and his lawyer friend and neighbor were walking across the street. They had their hands in their pockets, their heads were bowed in concentration or against the wind, and they were talking soberly. I had a swift feeling of certainty that they were discussing Dud. There was something secret, competent, in their manner. I was sure without knowing why that they were arranging protection against some threatened unpleasantness. Whatever it was, I never learned more than I knew from myself.

16

Return

I hadn't meant to go "home" to live with Mother when my husband went overseas in World War II. But with my father's death I felt I had to. My baby proved a distraction to her, and she wanted someone in the house. It wasn't a good time for either of us.

Probably it was Mother who suggested the visit to Atchison. The household was changed from my childhood, though Grandfather, in his eighties, still went downtown to his office. A nurse shared the Yellow Bedroom with Grandmother, who had developed a tendency to fall. Her breakfast was served on a tray, handpainted with yellow flowers, and gifts to Grandmother now were often a pretty embroidered mat and napkin set for the tray. The daintiest china was used, and in summer there was a flower from the garden.

The best attention could not compensate Grandmother for the loss of her former self. "Oh, Ellen," she said one day as I was sitting with her, "it's terrible to grow old." As I waited for some philosophical remark, she said, "Old people have so many *smells*." I'm afraid that I laughed.

My grandparents were delighted to have us come. There were still people to cook and clean and drive the car and do the laundry, and no one seemed to object to the extra work. Instead they seemed rather pleased at having new faces and topics of conversation in the house. Once again I became the companion of the current farm girl—Rosemary, now—who occupied the back bedroom. We both waited for overseas mail and shared with each other our worries at every change in military maneuvers. Grandmother, who had worried through the last war, was sympathetic but a little removed from this one. Mother was sunk in her own emotions, and Grandfather never expressed his reactions much anyway.

It was my uncle who began to relive his own war experiences and who seemed to understand my feelings. Once, gazing at the mirror surrounding the fireplace in his own living room, he mused—almost to himself, "One time we went into a chateau in France and there was a big beautiful mirror like that on one wall—all shattered. The Germans had smashed it with their gun butts just before they retreated." He shook his head. "It was too bad." And another time, looking at my toddler, "I'm glad I wasn't married when I went overseas. I'm glad I didn't have so much to leave."

For Mother, the visit was coming home to a protected time. She moved into the Pink Bedroom, which had originally been her nursery. I had my usual Blue Bedroom, with a crib set up by the high walnut footboard for my small son. Mother's girlhood friends came to call and to sympathize and tell her what a beautiful marriage she and Frederick had had. They hadn't seen much of the marriage, except for short visits, since my parents had moved from Atchison twenty-two years earlier. After each such expression, Mother said tearfully, "That's a comfort to me."

Atchison worked its old spell of timelessness on me. I don't know how long we stayed. I was willing to be soothed and comforted, too, but I kept being pulled into the present. The worry was always there.

The big cabinet radio in the living room had been used mainly for Grandfather's pleasure. He listened to the grain quotations and in the evenings chuckled over "Amos 'n Andy" while the rest of us tiptoed. Now I was the one who crouched in front of it. Every night I caught William L. Shirer's newscast. What new danger had the day brought?

Atchison had always been a great place for entertaining. Long before my birth, Grandmother had belonged to the exclusive Friday Afternoon Club. The most genteel and intelligent ladies of the town met in each others' homes for consumption of cake and Shakespeare.

When I visited, the children of Mother's girlhood friends were my companions. Sometimes we simply went to each others' homes to play. But sometimes, as we grew older, we gave each other "luncheons" in Gilbert's Tea Room, the ice cream parlor of my parents' courting days. (My favorite menu was a toasted, roasted almond sandwich—I liked to say it almost as much as I liked to eat it—and a Swiss chocolate sundae. The latter was ice cream covered with a thick, light chocolate sauce which I have never found again, even in Switzerland.) Or we went to matinees at one of the two movie theaters, where the bill was changed every two or three days.

My parents didn't much approve of movies. My father thought they were mostly "trash," and when I was a child I didn't go much at home. But the theaters were beginning to be "air-cooled" and offered respite from the Kansas heat, and so in Atchison I was introduced to the glamorous John Boles and Lily Damita and to Al Jolson singing "Sonny Boy." I was told by my friends that the real Sonny Boy had *really* died, just like in the movie.

Mother and Grandmother had parties, too. Sometimes they had luncheons at Grandmother's house where "the girls," dressed in the flowered georgette that stuck to their warm, talcumed backs, purred over me as I passed the pastel-colored mints. (These luncheons usually took place on a day when Grandfather went to Rotary.

Other days he came home for the noonday meal and for a short nap, sitting upright in his tufted leather chair before going back to the office.) Or on other occasions Mother and Grandmother went to parties, given by the same "girls" in their homes.

But things were different now. Mother and Grandmother weren't entertaining any more. Most of my childhood friends were no longer there. They were grown up and gone—to war jobs or to follow their husbands in service. At least the lucky ones were.

This visit I seldom if at all saw any of the girls with whom I used to have doll tea parties under the mulberry tree in Grandmother's front yard. Instead I became introduced to a new "crowd," those just too old for military service, those whose lives were minimally disrupted by the war, those who, in the main, now determined the course of Atchison life. These were the persons whom my uncle and aunt saw, though most of them were younger. (Mother said Mavis was always finding a new, young crowd to run with and that she had taken up with a new set of friends every time Mother was there. Mother said it was because no one could take Mavis for very long. *Mother's* friends, on the other hand, were those she had grown up with.)

I became aware of a strange preoccupation with the past in Atchison. At home I had grown up in a suburb several generations old, still inhabited by descendants of some of the original families. But ours was only one of the satellite communities around the central city. My parents had friends throughout the area, and I was not bounded by the town in which I went to school. The larger world of my father who, as a corporation lawyer, traveled the country, was to some extent mine too. What one did or was now was more important than what one's origins might be.

But in Atchison it was different. One seemed as responsible for one's antecedents as for oneself. One was somehow judged by what they had been.

I became aware of that at one luncheon. Mother's girlhood friend, Cecile Henry, though now an expatriate who never came to Atchison, was still drawing on her early background in her writing. She had just published another novel. It dealt, I heard, with two brothers married to two sisters. In Cecile's book there was an indication that the sisters had murdered their husbands for their money. Two of Grandmother's brothers, both dead now (one before my birth) had married two sisters who subsequently divorced them, gaining large settlements. Both women were said to be "fast"; one had even carried on with someone in Hollywood! The whispers around Atchison were that those two marriages had been the basis for Cecile's novel.

It all seemed a little remote to me. That is, until someone at the party, waiting until I was surrounded by a good-sized group, asked with disarming innocence, "What do you think of Cecile Henry's latest book?"

I said I hadn't read it. There were smug looks all around. I began to realize that I wasn't supposed to hold my head too high, because of something some deceased great-aunts-by-marriage whom I had never met had been imagined to do.

Saturday night parties were the most important. For one thing, the men were there. But mainly Saturday night was the night you were *supposed* to have a good time. So people greeted one another with great enthusiasm, even though they had all been together at another house last Saturday and had probably seen each other throughout the week. And they shrieked with laughter to prove that they were having fun. Why should I distrust this frantic gaiety? Perhaps they *were* having fun, perhaps this ebullience came from high spirits. But it seemed to me to be an effort to prove something to themselves, first of all, and to everyone else next. What did they need to prove? That their lives were full and enjoyable? That they had enough?

One such party was at the Mitchells'. They lived in a big red gingerbread house next door to the one in which Dud and my Other Grandmother had lived before my Other Grandmother had died and Dud had moved away. As I waited on the porch for the bell to be answered, I looked curiously at the house. From where I stood it seemed completely unfamiliar, as if I had never been there at all.

The party was given by someone I hardly knew. She was the married daughter of the house, home to wait out her husband's overseas service. Her brother, Bill Mitchell, was about my age, but he too was off in the service. The guests for the most part were the older Atchison group, already noisy and joyous as I entered. Unable to face so much enthusiasm right away, I sought out Mr. Mitchell in his little study off the front hall. He was surprised, pleased, and flattered when I introduced myself, never dreaming, poor man, that I wasn't being Elizabeth Henley's well-brought-up little daughter making obligatory obeisance to my nominal host, but that I really preferred his company to that in the loud hallway.

"*Elizabeth's* daughter! How nice of you to leave the party to speak to me!" He held my hand and smiled shyly. I thought him a quiet, gentle man. Mother had said that Harvey Mitchell, as a young man, had made a lot of money, and though he tried hard to be nice, he was a little untutored. Once he took Mother to the theater and embarrassed her by bringing along a box of chocolates. Mother knew that it wasn't proper to eat candy in the theater, but Harvey was meaning to please her, so she took off a kid glove and ate just *one* piece so he wouldn't think he had done anything wrong. A lady must always be considerate of other people's feelings, Mother said, even if sometimes you had to overlook a rule a little bit.

I couldn't stay forever in the study. Mr. Mitchell himself with great solicitude saw to it that I "go have a good time with the young people." So I mingled, laughing at jokes I didn't understand because they were based on current local happenings, drinking—or holding—drinks I didn't much want, dancing with people who didn't matter to me one way or the other.

Another young war wife was there. Who she was or who her husband was I didn't know. They hadn't been married long, and he was overseas. "I have faith in him!" she was protesting rather desperately as I approached the group. "No matter how long he's gone!"

There were chuckles and wise looks around her. Another war wife said, "I asked just one thing of my husband when he left." We waited. "Call her by my name in the morning." The acme of sophistication. Assenting murmurs from the listeners.

"But I *know* my husband will be faithful to me!" the other young wife cried, close to tears.

I was in the circle now. The others turned to me for a comment.

"It's hard enough to know about oneself, let alone someone else," I said. Nods of general approval. I had gained acceptance. But I moved on thinking, *You coward.* I could have given the young woman the agreement she needed. For I, too, was sure of someone.

Peyton Mills was there without his wife. I had never met him before, but I felt somewhat familiar with him because he was related to Mother's friends, Aunt Florence and Uncle Charles Mills. He was also, as I managed to sort out, the cousin of the absent husband of the Mitchell daughter who was giving the party. So he was somehow a known quantity, I thought. I decided to talk to him, as he was alone. The father of four, he seemed safely domesticated. After a while he suggested that we go into the pantry with another couple to get more ice for our drinks.

The four of us stood leaning against the old oak counters, making conversation. Suddenly, the lights went out. No one laughed or gasped or made a sound. But against my mouth was a moist, insistent one, smelling of bourbon. And a wet, probing tongue forced my lips apart.

I can't say that I handled the matter at all deftly. I was so surprised that I just stood there, stunned, for a moment. Then I broke away and made for the lighted hallway. I moved into the crowd in the living room. Soon Peyton and the others emerged from the pantry, looking as if nothing had happened. Really, nothing much had. But the sudden darkness (who had been next to the light switch? not Peyton) and the conspiratorial silence made me feel that they had all been cooperating to dupe me. I was repelled, furious, shaken.

I looked around until I saw Mother's cousin, Bill Graham, dancing in his socks on the polished hardwood floor. "Bill, run me home, would you? I have a headache."

Bill didn't argue. He said, "Let me find my shoes. I'll meet you at the door."

In the front hall I said my good-byes to my hostess. I could tell she didn't believe in my headache, but by that time I was really beginning to get one. Peyton appeared and said smoothly, "When my wife is feeling better, we'll hope to have you over."

"I'd love to see your children," I said and went down the porch steps with Bill. In the car he said, "That's a crowd that knows each other pretty well. Sometimes when they have a few drinks, they get a little—relaxed. Doesn't mean anything."

I murmured something. But I wondered how many of them were in on the little plot, and whether it was an episode to be talked over at the next Atchison party.

The porch light was on at Grandmother's house. I turned it off in the vestibule, dimly lit by the light coming through the etched glass door from the front hall. Everything was quiet in the house, and only the downstairs light and its twin in the upstairs hall were burning. I tiptoed into the Blue Bedroom and undressed quietly by the light coming from the hall so as not to wake my baby. Then I went down the corridor to the family bathroom beyond Grandfather's bedroom. I scrubbed my lips fiercely with a rough wash cloth. Then I stood at the brown marble basin and brushed my tongue with some of Grandfather's gritty tooth powder. I brushed so hard that it hurt. I found some mouthwash in the closet next to the basin and rinsed my mouth, spitting into the toilet. I was still shaky and furious, furious with Peyton (did he think that because my husband was overseas I was fair game?), furious with *Them* for uniting against me, furious with myself for doing whatever I had done to allow it all to happen (what *had* I done?) and furious most of all for making so much out of nothing. For it was nothing, I told myself. You're not a schoolgirl. Why are you reacting this way?

I made my way back to my room, past the Red Bedroom where Grandfather snored, past the Yellow Bedroom where Grandmother and her nurse lay, past the Pink Bedroom where Mother evidently slept, although she said she didn't sleep well now. I turned out the two sets of hall lights from the upstairs switch and entered my room without needing to see the way. I reached in the crib to feel my sleeping baby, peaceful and secure under the soft blanket. Then I climbed into the high old walnut bed. I settled gratefully into the familiar declivities of the mattress. The short wooden arms which extended along my pillow seemed to bend protectively around me. It was not until I pulled one of Grandmother's quilts up under my chin that I was able to let out a deep sigh and feel the knots inside me begin to loosen.

What had really upset me most was that such things weren't supposed to happen here, not so close to Grandmother's house.

·:·   ·:·   ·:·

"Why don't you move to Atchison until the war is over, Ellen?" said my aunt Mavis. "There's such a nice group of girls here. We play bridge several days a week. We could have such fun."

The idea appalled me. On several counts. I knew those "girls" of Mavis's. They were absolute demons when it came to cards. I didn't care for bridge very much. My father had spoiled it for me at the outset, insisting that I learn contract before I was interested, because it was a "civilized game." It was very unnerving to play with him. He insisted that he knew where every card in the deck was from the moment that the hands were dealt, and I believed him. If one hesitated before playing, he would explode, "I don't know what's holding you up. There's only one card you could play." And once you played, he usually said, "*That* wasn't it."

Once he rode the same train that some of my friends and I were taking back to college, and we got up a game in his compartment. He pulled his usual act on me. I knew what he wanted me to play, but I didn't have it. For the only time that I had ever witnessed, my father had miscounted. But when the hand was over, and I defended myself with, "See! I didn't have it!" he sulked and acted as if it were my fault that I didn't.

But it wasn't just the prospect of bridge that deterred me. It was the new view I was getting of Atchison. I was seeing the intrigue and the crosscurrents for the first time.

"She's having an affair," said my aunt Mavis of one of the "girls" in the "crowd," not one of my mother's friends, but one of Aunt Mavis's new young set. "Right under her husband's nose. And he's married too. A business associate of her husband's. He comes into town now and then. She sent him a telegram this last time saying 'Of course you'll stay with us,' and signed her name—*and her husband's!*"

"Do they do it there, in her house?" I asked.

"I don't know. But we're not used to things like that here. A little party flirting, maybe. But not an *affair*! They'll be at the party tonight. Take him away from her, Ellen. You're younger. It would serve her right."

I had no idea how you took anyone away from someone else, or what you would do with him once you had him. And I couldn't believe that Aunt Mavis would really approve the consequences of such an act.

"Watch them tonight," said Aunt Mavis. "You'll *see*!"

What I saw was a moderately attractive middle-aged pair being carefully, formally polite with each other. They were both kind and reasonably attentive to me as the young war wife with a baby, someone worthy of consideration. Certainly their public behavior was blameless. It was a fairly boring party.

The Atchison of my childhood had been one kind of place, one into which I could fit comfortably. It had been a world created by my grandparents two generations earlier, one maintained by my mother as she returned to Grandmother's house. But that place didn't exist now, not as the mainstream life of the town. And I didn't see where I could fit.

I didn't really have a place of my own during those war years. Upon my marriage I had left my parents' house, defying and denying the pattern that they had wanted me to live out. I had turned from my girlhood home more definitely than many did on marrying. Nowhere would seem like mine until I could again establish my separate home, preferably with my husband, but essentially living by methods of my own choosing. Although Mother's house in our St. Louis suburb certainly didn't supply that freedom, it was at least located in an area where I had friends.

They were in the main the girls I had grown up with. Although many of us had gone away to college, we shared a common base of the past and the concerns of the present. For the most part, we knew each other's husbands. That was a comfort, because we had the incessant desire to talk about those absent men with someone who knew them. We were back in our parents' homes again, unwillingly, knowing among ourselves that we were not the same young women who had lived there only a few years ago, even if our parents did not see the change. We understood each other. We could express—or knew without saying—our mutual worries and the frustrations of separation. And we were rubbed raw by what we saw as the infuriating insensitivities of our mothers, most of whom had never experienced what we were experiencing now. They, in turn, were bewildered and irritated at the difficulty of reincorporating their daughters into their old places in the households which the mothers were still attempting to run in their accustomed way.

And my husband's family was near. On pleasant afternoons when my baby was up from his nap, I would put him in his stroller and wheel him the two-and-a-half blocks to my in-laws' house. We were always welcome. While we visited, my father-in-law would return from the office, delighted to see us. Nowhere else could I find such enthusiasm for the excerpts of letters I shared, nowhere else was my worry so understood when the mail stopped or new military action was reported, and nowhere else were my relief and jubilation met with such smiles.

One August afternoon I took my baby for the familiar visit. It was my wedding anniversary. Mother hadn't been aware of the date, but both my parents-in-law met me at the back door as we entered. My mother-in-law began to tell me how glad they were to have me in the family, and how they hoped that on the next anniversary, my husband and I would be together. My father-in-law stood and beamed, letting her speak for them both. Suddenly I, who seldom turned to tears—even at night on my pillow—felt a sob rise and fled into the little bedroom off the pantry. My father-

Grandmother and Grandfather Henley, Elizabeth, Ellen, and baby

in-law, still smiling, but obviously uncomfortable, reached for my child's hand and led him away. The men would depart, leaving the emotions to the women! After I had calmed myself, I emerged to find my mother-in-law waiting in the kitchen. She gave me a Coke and stood with me while I drank it.

"You know, Ellen," she said, "you wouldn't be given this to bear if you hadn't the strength to endure it."

I didn't believe her for one second.

Always, when it was time to go, my father-in-law would put on his hat and push the stroller back home for me, in order to talk a little longer. Often he was so involved with his side of the conversation that he missed the cutoff between the streets and went on an extra half block before turning. I usually felt it best to let him talk without interruption.

"I miss him," he said of my husband, who was in business with him in civilian life. "He used to come into my office, and we'd talk. So many little things . . ."

Although it had been Mother's idea to come to Atchison in the first place, I think things didn't work out so well for her there, either. She was in a terrible trap. She was two persons at once. On the one hand, everything in her cried out to be once again the protected daughter she had been in her youth, when Grandmother's house was home. But that home, as she had known it, no longer existed. And she felt the competing onus of the returning daughter of the house, the one who would take charge and protect her elderly parents. She didn't want to be either one exclusively. Yet she couldn't give up either role. She had Grandmother as the model of a devoted daughter, one who had constantly run up the hill to answer Great-grandmother's whims. Probably Mother felt that her mother expected the same treatment from her. Ever a nervous person, trying to convince herself that she was doing her duty, Mother was now even more apt to make issues out of small matters. The maid Rosemary and the nurse in particular began to go around looking thin-lipped.

And Mother continually got crosswise with Mavis, whom she had never liked or approved of anyway. When, as a small child, I had announced delightedly that I knew a flapper, my aunt Mavis, who rolled her stockings below her knee, Mother sniffed and said you weren't *supposed* to be a flapper once you were married. Aunt Mavis said to Mother that the expenses at Grandmother's house were ridiculous. There were the nurse and someone to cook and clean and a laundress besides that and someone to drive the car and someone for the yard and garden in the summer. It didn't make sense to have so many to take care of just two people. Mother said that it was Grandfather's and Grandmother's money and that *she* wasn't trying to save it to inherit, even though she no longer had a husband to support her. And anyway, Mavis was a fine one to object to extravagance!

Probably another reason for Mother's resentment was that I began to see Aunt Mavis as a friend. When we had come to Atchison for my father's funeral a few months earlier, my husband, on emergency leave from his port of embarkation, our baby, and I had stayed at my uncle's house while Mother stayed at Grandmother's house. Mavis and Graham had been quietly aware of the weight of our emotions, our need to make the most of those few unexpected days together in the midst of shock and sorrow. Mavis, without saying much, had relieved me of some of the child-care duties so that we could have some time alone. Graham had driven us to the junction in Armour, where my husband caught the connecting train for Kansas City and then a plane back to his point of departure for overseas. Graham paced down the cindered railroad siding so that we could have those last choked farewell moments in privacy. From his experiences as an artillery officer in his war, he knew what might lie ahead.

Back in Atchison again, I found empathy from Mavis. She knew that Mother could be a difficult person; she had had reason to learn that over the years. She told me how once she had been sick at home alone, and my father had brought her some flowers. He came and sat by her bed and talked to her. She said that she had been feeling low, and he had cheered her up. But when "they," my mother and grandmother, found out about it, they'd made a big fuss and had told him that he had done a terrible thing, going into the bedroom like that with no one else in the house. It hadn't been like that at all, she said. They had had the nicest conversation.

Mavis invited me to small dinner parties with their friends. I
don't recall what Mother did on those evenings, but she wasn't
there. And sometimes Mavis and I would simply take a walk together. We both did some talking then. I learned that it wasn't so
easy to be Grandmother's daughter-in-law, at least not in the same
town. When Mavis called in an architect and remodeled the house
which she and Uncle Graham had bought from my grandfather—
the house in which I had been born—she took a lot of criticism
from my grandparents. They thought she was too extravagant.
Mavis said they talked about the money, but really they never
wanted to change *anything*. She had certainly changed a lot, ripping
off the wraparound porch, throwing the two front rooms together,
reversing the positions of the dining room and kitchen, and tearing
out the back stairs. I secretly mourned the loss of things that I had
remembered, but I had to admit that Mavis had created a handsome, modern house.

"It isn't easy to move into Atchison," Mavis told me. "They keep
reminding you that you don't quite belong. I've been here—how
long?—more than twenty years—and I'm still an outsider. I expect
if Jack Blake and his wife settle here after the war, she'll find that
too."

"Oh, is Jack married?"

"Yes, a girl from out West he met during his army training.
Mildred acts delighted about it now, but if they live here for good,
it may be a different story. Little things, you know. Everybody
knows everything you do. And they all have an opinion!"

When I came back from those encounters, Mother would say
jealously, her sharp nose seeming almost to twitch, "What did you
and Mavis talk about?"

"Raising boys," I would answer. "Places they took their boys on
vacations." As Mother had no boys, she couldn't enter too much

into such a discussion. I was perfectly truthful. We *did* talk about my cousins, but we talked about other things too.

The difficulty for Mother, of course, was that her parents had grown old. They had been old for a long time, but while my father lived that hadn't been a problem. He had been both leader and buffer in the larger world they entered after Atchison. My father gave Mother an "allowance." Mother said Daddy was "generous"; she said he said she was "good" about not overspending, not like some women. She ran the house well and entertained graciously. He put assets in her name (perhaps in another's as well) and died without a will.

My grandparents were saddened that Mother was widowed, but they had entered the stage of remoteness from life's problems. Grandfather, known throughout his life as a shrewd money man, reiterated his old rules: "Never sell your mill stock," and "Don't go into capital." (She eventually did both.) He had no notion of the value—or lack thereof—of the big house that she and my father had bought during the prosperous twenties and happily converted with an oil heating system some years later. Now with wartime oil rationing, it was impossible to keep warm. The many high-ceilinged rooms, leaking heat through their open archways, were not an attraction to potential buyers. Grandfather couldn't imagine that the house would actually bring less than my father paid for it, and that Mother would have to pay more for a smaller house which would be maintained without a large domestic staff. *He* still had loyal household help, and he couldn't understand that things were different in St. Louis. Mother began to realize that she could not regard her father as an infallible source of advice. At fifty-four, she suddenly had to grow up. It was a realization that terrified and crushed her, one that she never came to terms with.

⋰ ⋰ ⋰

It was time to leave Atchison. As usual Rosemary drove the Hudson to the railroad crossing at the mill because the parlor car stopped there. The station farther down the track received the engine and was a long walk from our section. Also as usual, Grandfather, though loath to have us go, saw that we made the five-minute trip from the house to the train half an hour before the scheduled departure time, just to be sure. He walked restlessly up and down the sidewalk, pausing to greet by name the mill workmen, dusty with flour, who left their noisy machines to speak to him. When the train arrived he hustled us aboard as soon as the conductor put down the step.

We were still settling ourselves in the compartment which we had been able to reserve so that my baby could nap during part of the day when a smiling face appeared at the door. It was Jack Blake, my childhood hero, handsome in his officer's uniform.

"Hi! We saw you get on. Joyce is here with me." This last was said proudly. They had spent a few days' leave with his parents, and now he was returning to his post. The train was crowded, as wartime trains usually were, and we asked them to share our compartment as far as Kansas City where they were to change trains.

Jack and Joyce seated themselves close together opposite Mother and me. I saw and understood and was glad for them. Jack was as nice a man as the boy I remembered. What seemed so odd was the realization that we were both grown up now. He was no longer the older boy, the baseball hero impossibly remote from me. He was, I realized, only the age of my own husband. We were for the first time contemporaries.

Jack played with my little boy who, missing his abruptly absent father and grandfather, responded in delight to this affectionate man. Jack picked him up. Holding him on his lap, he smiled at me. "The war will be over and his daddy will be back with him soon," he said reassuringly. I wanted to believe him, so I did. He was right, although it was nineteen more months before his proph-ecy came true. But Jack's presence, his cheerfulness, his unspoken assurance that we all cared for each other lifted our spirits.

Sealed into that little compartment, rocking along beside the Missouri River, we were all embarked on journeys that would test us and in the end separate us. We would all survive the war which so filled the consciousness of three of us. But other dangers were ahead. Some of us would be overtaken. Jack and Joyce, seated so close to each other now, wouldn't stay married. After the war Joyce would take the children they had produced, return to her family in the West, and divorce Jack. He, too, would leave Atchison. Far behind and unreachable would be the security of first-grade birth-day parties, of triumphs on the baseball diamond, of warm tears of affection at a wedding. Somehow those days could no longer protect him. Jack, who now sat opposite to me, handsome and healthy, would become an alcoholic. He would be nearly killed in a car accident and lose his job. Later he would remarry and one Sunday morning, mowing his lawn in an Oklahoma town, he would drop dead of a heart attack. I learned of all that from my uncle, years after both Jack and I had left Atchison. Sometimes I wondered if Jack had been on the way to finding again that safeness, lost since childhood. After the torment, perhaps he was creating a happy ending after all. Or a new beginning.

My small son would, of course, grow up and leave me. He would establish new loyalties and meet new challenges. His ability to leave—and those carefully nurtured steps along the way to inde-pendence—would be in part my design and doing. Then I would no longer be able to soothe his hurts and fears. I would not even know of most of them. He would be a man responsible for himself.

He would also be a father, cautiously urging his own son to independence. He would learn the fears of a parent, and he would know what it is to miss a child. He would worry when his nine-year-old son made his first plane flight alone to visit me. He would need the reassurance of several phone conversations during his child's brief absence. He would discover bit by bit how parents become dispensable. And he would experience the poignant mix of pride and the yearning after a child whose feet are set firmly on a path of his own. Would he also know that I might have—along with my pride—a similar yearning after him? Probably not.

And Mother and I—Mother and I . . . Already we were separate from each other. We would continue to be bound by duty and custom rather than by the rapport of two truly compatible persons. I would eventually know some of what she was going back to face as a widow. But I would have that break in my life at an earlier age.

Even then my emotions would not be the same as Mother's. The break forced on her by death was one which she sometimes seemed to reinforce by choice. When finally we moved from my childhood home, she left behind much of my father's past. He had made a library table for their first bungalow and a lamp to go on that table. The mahogany lamp base was a copy of one of his old Missouri University columns. Perhaps he was seeking to bring one of his old loyalties into his new life. He brought nothing from his mother's house. But these talismans of promises unkept went to the new owners of the house. Without my own home, I had no place in which to save them. They weren't a style I admired, but so much pride and anticipation must have gone into the making!

On one last hopeless circuit of the attic, still partially decorated with remnants of a long-ago Halloween party of mine, I found the little gold-framed picture of my Other Grandparents, of Dud and my father as children, with Uncle Henry and the first Adelia. Mother knew it was there. Abandoning it was her last gesture of rejection. Secretly I packed it in a suitcase.

∴   ∴   ∴

So we went back to Mother's house. With our knowledge that we would soon be moving, we imbued it with our sense of leave-taking. We couldn't seem to settle in again, although we saw more than a year's change of seasons before the house was sold. Mother hadn't been happy there for the last years of her marriage, and I had left in my own mind long before I made a reluctant, physical return. It didn't feel like home to either of us.

But then neither did Grandmother's house.

17

Endings

My trips to Atchison were only for funerals now. Grandmother's first and, after a three-year sentence of bewildered loneliness, Grandfather's. The household was broken up. The dining room furniture, always understood to be destined for my mother, did, indeed, come to her. By that time, she had sold the big house in which I had grown up and was through with the formal dinner parties she and my father used to give when the guests "dressed" for dinner, when settings for twelve around the oval table began with service plates, the gold-encrusted ones with the floral center, or the gray-and-white with a half-inch sterling silver rim.

Mother became more reclusive herself. There were times I almost said, to jolt her back to life, "You're getting to be like another Mrs. Paulsen, aren't you?" It might have worked. It might have been the only challenge to rouse her. But I was neither cruel nor courageous enough to try.

One more funeral. Calling home from London, where I had accompanied my husband on a business trip, I learned that Mother had died. She had been ailing for years. But so had my grandmother Henley, and she had lived until she was eighty-seven. Mother was seventy-one. The difference, perhaps, was that Grandmother had Grandfather acting as an anxious buffer between her and isolation. She hadn't had to turn to herself alone for strength.

We made our final arrangements by long distance. My uncle,

now retired in California, agreed to meet us in Atchison. We would place Mother's body where she felt home to be. She would be safe again with her parents, once more their protected little daughter.

At the mortuary a sweet-faced woman approached me. "Do you know who I am?"

"Why—Mrs. Childress!" And, to my husband, "Mrs. Childress lived next door to Mother and Daddy here. She taught Mother to diaper me." (When I was small I had, for a time, thought she was Mrs. "Children" because she had so many.)

"That's right." She smiled and held my hands. "I've been to see your auntie."

"My—auntie?" The only aunt I thought of, my uncle's wife, Mavis, was in California and had not accompanied him to the funeral.

"Your father's sister. She's in the hospital. She's had a stroke."

"Oh—she has?" Was I supposed to do something? Feel something? What I felt was surprise. Dud had a friend. A nice, normal woman. How could that be?

In the funeral car, I must have mentioned the encounter. The funeral director at the wheel mused, "She had the most beautiful speaking voice I ever heard in a woman."

She spoke, then. Someone heard her. She must at times have spoken pleasantly. I tried vainly to recapture that voice, but my memory was blank. I remembered my father's emphasis on a woman's speaking voice, how pleased he was that mine was low. Both he and my mother felt that her voice was inclined to shrillness.

My uncle had arranged for us to stay in the home of the Mitchells, a couple whom I didn't really know. I had never met the wife. Bill, the husband, and I were about the same age. I had a vague recollection of having attended some of the same children's parties as he did on my early visits to Atchison, but we hadn't seen each other for years. It had been in his parents' home that I had attended that wartime party, given by his sister. But Bill himself had been away in service then.

Over drinks before dinner, Bill looked at me thoughtfully and then seemed to make up his mind. "You know, my parents' house was right next door to your grandmother Paulsen's."

I had known.

"She and her daughter used to make special cookies and call the neighbor children in."

"They *did?*"

"They were—strange people. But they were awfully good cooks."

My view of my other grandmother's world was enlarging. I was seeing her and Dud as more in touch with other human beings than I had ever supposed them to be. It was as if a censor's ban had been lifted, and people felt a need to tell me something.

I went to bed exhausted and fell into a heavy sleep, but sometime later I found myself completely awake in the dark. Jet lag, of course. I was still on London time. Tired, but unable to sleep I lay in the strange room, facing the dark of the window. A faint glow, the reflected moonlight off the Missouri River somewhere below the house, gave a little light. Three o'clock thoughts crowded in.

My mother had died with only strangers near. Had she been afraid? Mother was a fearful person. Did she have a hand to hold at the last?

Across the town from me in the hospital on the hill, Dud now lay dying. Could Mother's experience with death give her—wherever she might be—compassion for Dud, the fellow feeling that neither had had for the other? Could I loosen the old prohibitions imposed by loyalty to my mother? Did she now give me permission?

I turned on my side. The time for punishment was past. I knew what I would do.

∴   ∴   ∴

I was sure she would be up early, and she was. She answered the phone on the second ring. "Mrs. Childress?" I said, standing in the downstairs library of a strange house, speaking almost secretly before anyone else was awake. "This is Ellen."

"*Yes*, dear!" She seemed to have been waiting for my call. Her voice was warm and creamy, the voice that had soothed my mother's fears when I was a baby, the voice that crooned to children, the voice she must now take to the hospital to comfort my aunt.

Clumsily, the words not sounding right, I told her what I had in mind. She was not surprised. Mrs. Childress needed no explanation. "I'll make the arrangements, dear."

After breakfast I borrowed a car and drove to Mrs. Childress's house. She still lived next door to the house that had been my uncle's. I had been born in the front bedroom with Dr. Charley working furiously, plunging me, I was told, first into a tub of hot water and then one of cold, finally hitting me in the face with a knotted wet towel to make me cry and breathe.

It was to Mrs. Childress that Mother ran, panicky, with me in her arms when I rocked too hard in my high chair and tipped over, hitting my head. Mrs. Childress with a large brood of her own, Mrs. Childress, the calm, the capable. And now here she was again when needed, neat in her well-brushed black coat and hat, some late fall asters wrapped in a cone of damp newspapers. "I thought we could just take these," she said, smiling as she seated herself in the car.

She was known at the hospital. She spoke to the man mopping the floor as we entered, to the woman at the desk, to the nurses we passed in the corridor. She presented me to the floor nurse in charge, "Miss Paulsen's niece, just back from London," which seemed to excuse any neglect on my part, hinted, even, that I was flying in to deal with the crisis.

The nurse rose, eager to preside at the meeting.

"That's all right, dear, I know the way. Thank you for letting us come before the regular hours."

Down the hall, past breakfast trays still on carts, past open doors until we came to one that was closed. "Here, dear," and Mrs. Childress opened the door and edged me in.

The room was bright, glaring, shiny. There were two beds in the room, but only one was occupied. Mrs. Childress urged me forward until I had to look at the figure on the bed.

It was, I knew, a woman. But the face was heavy and sexless. The grayed dark hair was splayed, wild but lifeless, on the pillow. The jaw, nose and cheekbones were prominent. White, inward curving hairs grew on the chin, and a dark, faint mustache smudged the upper lip. I couldn't superimpose the face I had dimly seen one long-ago summer afternoon on this one. I searched the features, striving for something familiar, trying to find the life behind them. What, in her, was my father? Where was I?

"Dud, dear," said Mrs. Childress gently, "here is Frederick's daughter. This is your niece. This is Ellen."

The large dark eyes turned in my direction. They paused, near but not quite on my face. I cleared my throat. "Hello, Aunt Dud." I was the only one who had the right to call her that. But she hadn't wanted to hear it, years ago. It sounded so out of place and forced—so intimate where no intimacy had existed—that I felt I should add something.

"I'm your brother's daughter." I remembered the childhood nickname. "Fritzi's daughter." Still the dark eyes, turned in my direction. No life moved in them. I thought she must have a sort of visual aphasia, that the meaning of objects perceived by the eye did not register in the brain. Mrs. Childress was quiet, watching. My words sounded sparse and chill. Mrs. Childress seemed to expect something.

"She can't speak, you know," she whispered.

We confronted each other, my aunt and I. I felt the obligation—to whom?—to make some gesture that she could comprehend. Tentatively, with some revulsion, I took her hand. I felt Mrs. Childress behind me relax.

The hand was my father's, long-fingered, slender, an aristocratic hand, he always claimed, when he observed my version. It was inert and cool. I covered it with my other hand. And I stood there, uncomfortable, not knowing how to shift position or let go.

Mrs. Childress approached the bed. "There, there, dear, don't cry," she said to Dud. With tenderness she blotted the two tears just spilling from the clouded eyes. "We'd best go now. We don't want to tire her," she said to me. Then, mother to us both, she patted Dud's bristly cheek and guided me to the hall and release.

The door closed behind me. The last door. Speechless, Dud—her memories of my grandparents, my father, herself as a child—was locked away from me forever.

Gaining the parking lot, safe in the car, I had to restrain my impulse to roll up the windows and lock the doors. I felt that we had passed through a danger, one that could still reach out and permeate my life. For a few moments I sat without turning on the ignition. Mrs. Childress waited quietly beside me.

At last she said, "She's had several strokes, you know." Her calm voice defined reality again and brought me once more into a world that one could recognize, where one could act rationally. I felt that I had been shudderingly close to an unmanageable irrationality.

"She has?"

"Yes." Mrs. Childress settled herself comfortably, seeming to consider it not at all strange that we sat in an unmoving car in a hospital parking lot, even though our errand was over. "The first time, it was her legs, but she could still speak. They brought her here then. And when I was just leaving after the first visit, do you know what she said to me?"

"What?"

"She said, 'Did you see the pretty slippers that Fritzi gave to me?'"

"*Fritzi?*" A cold hand from the realm of the irrational reached out to me again and touched the back of my neck.

"Your father."

"Yes, I know. But what—?"

"Of course, he's been dead too long for her to still have anything from him. It was the stroke. She was confused, you see. That happens."

"But they hadn't had anything to do with each other for years before he died."

Mrs. Childress nodded. She was looking out of the car window toward a man raking leaves by the front walk to the hospital. A gust of wind whirled the leaves out of his pile as he built it. Perhaps the wind had made me cold. Then she said in a voice unlike her usual voice, in a voice suddenly tired and old, "She must have missed him very much all this time."

But now, who was left to tell me more? My uncle, writing laconically from California, said, "You may have heard they were crazy. *Not a bit of it.*" But he knew little of the background. He had been a player on the high school basketball team which my father coached around his law practice. His contact began when my father was a young man, just come to establish himself as an attorney in Atchison. What he knew of the break would have been my mother's interpretation.

Then I remembered. Some years earlier I had made a friend whose parents, I discovered, had known my father in his youth. I wrote, asking for information and memories of the family. The response was better than I had hoped: the name and address of my father's only living cousin, an unmarried woman living in Carrollton, Missouri, his boyhood home. A correspondence began, then finally she made us a visit.

Cousin Lillian, younger than my father in their childhood, but now, in her sixties, older than he had lived to be, was voluble and obviously the family genealogist. I got lost in the welter of my paternal relatives that crowded around our dinner table as she talked the first night of her visit. The daughter of my grandmother's brother, hers were mostly childhood memories and tales of my grandmother's family, the German side. Her view of my Danish grandfather, who died when she was a very small child, must have been colored by that family.

"He made a great deal of money, and he spent it all. He had the finest of everything in his saloon." (How like my father that sounded!) "He didn't leave Aunt Norma, your grandmother, at all well off."

I found myself defending a grandfather whom I had never known. Strangely, I actually felt an angry loyalty. "But he was only forty-eight when he died! And he had the saloon—a going business—"

"Aunt Norma didn't have a business head. And your father was only ten. She hired a manager and told him just to give her two hundred dollars a month—that's all she needed. He never accounted for the rest."

"But why didn't her brothers look into things? *They* had businesses and must have known—" I realized that Cousin Lillian's own father was one of those I was impugning.

"And then," she continued, "in a few years local option in Carroll County voted the saloon out of business—and she had nothing."

"But my grandfather could never have expected anything like

that to happen! He was a Dane! He probably thought beer was a permanently safe investment!"

Later I added, innocently, I hoped, "Daddy said his mother's mother and sister lived with them. Aunt Emma, wasn't it?"

"Yes. Later Emma married the man who managed the saloon. They were very well off. Emma was an old maid when she married," said Cousin Lillian comfortably. Never in her own sixty-plus un-married years had she felt herself an old maid.

The next morning, over second cups of coffee after the family had left, she said thoughtfully, "I see now. He had it all on him— the family, I mean. Uncle Paulsen, I'm talking about. Your grand-father."

I have cleared your name, I signaled to a listening shade.

"They moved to Atchison because of Uncle Henry, you know. After his wife, Adelia—the first Adelia—died. Your grandmother's sister, for whom Dud was named."

"Did my grandmother expect to marry Uncle Henry?"

"Dud. It was Dud. They had the same name, you see. And Dud was beauti—she *considered* herself beautiful. She was always posing. But Henry married someone else. He was so good to them! But they broke with him finally. I don't remember why."

Cousin Lillian kept me informed of trips and calls to Atchison caused by Dud's deteriorating condition. Dud never left the hos-pital where Mrs. Childress visited her and at last her life ended there.

Cousin Lillian wrote that she was arranging for burial in the family plot in Carrollton and for markers to be put up for Dud and her mother. The latter had never been done, perhaps because Dud couldn't afford it. "I want to share the expense with you," I wrote, and she replied, "*I never intended that!*" I was sure she

hadn't, but, remembering the slender stack of checks in the safe deposit box, I felt better at sharing.

Then came the dismantling of Dud's room. Did I want the walnut bedroom set? wrote Cousin Lillian. It had been my grandparents' and was in bad condition but could be refinished. Regretfully, I wrote no. It was massive, too large for my rooms, expensive to transport and recondition.

And yet it had been marriage bed for a marriage that had produced my father. I remembered his saying that when he was six years old, his father had taken him into the bedroom and seated him on the high bed—*that* one—while he explained the Free Silver issue and the Cross of Gold speech. But, no, I really couldn't use it.

But there were smaller things, contents of a bureau drawer, perhaps, that Cousin Lillian sent to me. One was an intricately knotted gold pin, enameled with blue-and-white flowers, centered with a diamond. Dud "always" wore it, wrote Cousin Lillian; her father had given it to her. So my Danish grandfather had loved his daughter and had chosen something to make her feel valued as a young girl nearing womanhood. What would have happened to her had he been around to value her as she became a young woman?

There were two rings, one a heavy gold wedding band with my grandparents' initials and the wedding date inscribed. But here— here in my hand was another gold ring with a rampant bear in a crest. "Our family crest," Cousin Lillian explained.

Strange. My father had told me of the German family crest from his mother's side, had even sketched it from memory, much as I saw it now. He told me he had owned a signet ring which he had worn until he went into service. The anti-German feeling with World War I had caused him to put it aside.

Aside? But his enlistment came *after* the break with his mother. Yet here was the ring in his sister's effects. Had he made a surreptitious farewell visit before going off to war? Were they all kind to each other for one last time?

Several sheets of something typed were folded together, fraying apart at the seams. I opened them carefully and pieced them together. "Agnostic Prayer," the title stated boldly. There followed many lines of poetry with crossings-out and additions in my father's writing. It was the self-dramatizing work of a young man, struggling with the imponderables of the universe. There was an unmistakable tone of personal admiration. The last page had my father's bold signature, not quite so stylized and sure as it later became but marked with the individuality which he must have been trying to develop. But at the very bottom of the last page, written in small letters in a different hand, was a date: January 8, 1912. That was probably the year of my parents' engagement, perhaps before it occurred. Did my father share his thoughts with

Dud as they grew up? Was she a confidante, displaced when he began to love another woman?

There was a sheet from the Atchison paper, dated about two years before Dud's death. A pencil check marks a column of nostalgia titled: "Forty Years Ago . . . August 1921." The last item recounts that my father, "assistant attorney general of Kansas . . . former city attorney of Atchison," had been appointed "assistant attorney" to the Telephone Company in St. Louis. The account appeared more than seventeen years after my father's death.

Then there was a photograph album. It must have been made in the family's early Atchison days, for there were pictures of my young father on the porch of the red brick house and some of him with a bulldog about which he had told me. There were some blank spaces with bits of photographic paper still sticking to the remnants of dried paste, as if something had been angrily ripped out. Could there have been photographs of my mother, destroyed when the reality they recorded persisted?

Here are pictures of Dud. Mother was right. She was a tremulously beautiful young woman with limpid dark eyes and a soft, yearning mouth. Where was that face in the face I last saw? What had destroyed that beauty? She destroyed it herself, a threatening voice in the back of my mind answered. Somehow she couldn't fight back the forces of destruction that we all—yes, that I—that I!—have in us.

And here is my other grandmother, standing erect beside her house, eyeing down the camera. I look at the face of the woman I never knew, never really saw in that dim room long ago, the woman who had somehow determined me.

It is not the face of a weakling. It is a strong face, a stern face, a handsome face. Here is the slim, straight nose of my father, the determined mouth. And, yes, here are the shadowed eyes with the

Dud

same dark circles under them that my father had when he was tired or sad—or gazing into impenetrable mysteries—that I have, that my youngest son has inherited.

So you are my grandmother. I have from you not the sunny curls of protected childhood where the greatest remembered tragedy was a thoughtless snip of a barber's shears, but the shadows under the eyes. Coming from what fatigue at the world's burdens, from what dark vision? Grandmother, grandmother, I call you that now as never I could. We are bound to each other and to the terrors we both see, the terrors my busy, nest-building grandmother never knew. We know that unknown horrors wait in the darkness. We glimpse the tiger crouching in the shadows, waiting to spring. Grandmother, I know you at last.

I look again at Dud's lovely young face, the face her father must have foretold when he chose the little brooch for her. I cannot see what is there behind it to turn it into the leftover woman with the ruined mind that I viewed on that hospital bed. That morning, I made her face me without the sustaining hatred that had been for her the focus of all those years. She had to look at me without the force that had been her strength.

But what strength have I? I have in me the same dark twisted force that would keep me from the world, from light, from human beings. I have looked and seared that face into my mind, the face of another who has seen the tiger.

And I know what I fear, what all of us who share this dark knowledge fear. It is what makes me run, into action, into causes, into human contact. As my father ran, ran to an early grave.

We run, my grandmother, my father, Dud and I, from the same specter. The specter that would imprison us behind the drawn blinds in the dark house. The specter that would bring us sightless, speechless, mindless—but not without terror—to a hospital bed, shipwrecked without a voyage.

18

Grandmother's House Revisited

Atchison again, and summertime.

We come off the bridge from the Missouri side, my son Duncan, his wife Jen, their children Connie and David, and I. At the foot of the bridge is the old mill office, a low red brick building. Across from it is the "new" mill office, built by my uncle during his term as president of the mill, beginning in 1929. Perhaps it was the visible sign of progress that a young executive needs. Now it bears the sign, "ROCKWELL CO."

The old mill office was always the first landmark I recognized on my visits to Grandmother's house. But today we are not making the same sort of visit. We are to meet my two cousins beside the grave of my uncle, their father. None of us has been to Atchison in over twenty years. Our last meeting here was at Grandfather's funeral.

We find the motel, "about five blocks down the road as you come off the bridge," just as the proprietor told me over the phone. The room which we have taken for the day so that the children can rest is raw-wood paneled and hot. I find the switch for the window air conditioner and hope that things will cool off for my daughter-in-law and the children while my son and I attend the service.

"The one thing I want to do," says my son, "is find Old Pep's grave."

Old Pep was my father, the grandfather whom my son never

182

knew. As coach of the high school basketball team, he enjoined his boys, "Get some more pep into it!" until one, who was to become my uncle, nicknamed him "Pep."

"Let me check in with the funeral director to see if the boys are here," I say.

The boys, Dick and Graham, Jr., are forty-six and fifty now. I make several tries to reach the mortuary by phone. Finally, "Is Mr. Henley there?"

"Does it make any difference which one you talk to?"

"No."

Dick comes on, and we confirm the time for the service. Dick says, "We thought we'd go to the cemetery now. We want to look for some old graves."

"That's just what *we* want to do."

"We're on our way."

When they come, introductions are necessary. It seems strange to see my son shaking hands with my cousins, all new to each other, but with much the same familial coloring. Graham, Jr., remembers to say that my grandchildren are attractive, but I know it feels odd for both of us that here, now, in this town I have grandchildren. He and I should be the children here.

We are none of us too sure of the way. Graham, Jr., and Dick left town for good when they began their business careers. My uncle and aunt retired to California shortly thereafter. My Atchison memories are based on a child's geography, in which you are picked up and put someplace without knowing how you got there. We leave Jen, smiling gamely, and the children, who have discovered a see-saw. I hope they won't be too hot. The boys lead the way, waiting at the turns, until here it is: Mount Vernon Cemetery. As we swing in between the big stone posts, Duncan says, "It looks just the way I wanted it to look in my mind. It looks just the way a Kansas cemetery *ought* to look."

We drive slowly, peering for the family plot. I was here on many a summer Sunday, playing among the family graves while Grandmother replaced the flowers with fresh ones from her garden. I hope my memory will take over as we wind up the gravel drive, that I can find the turns. By the time Graham points and then motions us to a parking place in the shade, we have seen it too, the big, solid granite marker saying simply, "Graham."

A canopy has been set up and a ground cloth spread. No one is around but two overalled workmen. We approach from the back of the monument.

"Oh," says Dick, "they've got Grandpa covered up." The cloth is over the slab.

"We can uncover it," says one of the workmen. "We wanted a place for the flowers. . ."

"Yeah, let's get him uncovered," Dick says. It is a slight shock to realize that he has been an executive in a large company, used to making quick decisions and speaking with authority, for more years than he was the little boy I knew.

We explore the gravesite. On one side are my parents, Frederick Werner Paulsen and Elizabeth Henley Paulsen, and Grandfather, Hiram Hamilton Henley, and Grandmother, Ellen Graham Henley.

"Ellen," says my son. "You got your name from her?" I thought he knew that.

The place for Graham, Sr., is next to Grandfather. On the other side of the marker lie Grandmother's parents, Margaret Eaton Graham and Edward Kimball Graham, and their four sons—but no wives! I realized that the sons were inclined to divorce, and I remember Great-grandmother Graham's reported admonition before Graham married Mavis: "All of the Graham men are lousy husbands, except for Old Ed." The opinion may have been hers, but the wording sounds like Graham, Sr., who, after all, told the story. The sons are there, Wesley, Will, Ed ("the doctor") and

Elwood, the youngest, always something of a troublemaker. Grand-mother's girlhood diary recounted, "Elwood ran away and I got blamed." Later he got Aunt Louisa in trouble until her brothers, the Patterson boys, found out and called on him. The wedding took place, and everyone in the family adored Aunt Louisa. Elwood continually caused problems at the Graham Milling Company, where he was not employed but enjoyed voting his stock in un-cooperative ways. Great-grandmother sided with him, and Grand-father was called upon to be the eternal peacemaker. Grandfather was fair and unimpassioned, and everyone listened to him.

Elwood's grave is slightly around the corner of the plot marker, in the shadow, as if he had been told to sit on a chair until he could say he was sorry. I seem to remember Grandmother—though the eldest child, she outlived her brothers—rather grimly placing him there. She couldn't deny him his rightful position, but she could still discipline him a little. I point his grave out to Graham, Jr., and mention that Elwood is said to have been born because the rubber broke. Graham nods in confirmation. My son says later that it was evidently common family knowledge.

It is a blazing Kansas summer day. A half hour before high noon, the sun beats out of a brilliant sky, and nearly a hundred degrees of dry heat pour around us. But there are big trees and shade and a hot breeze.

"We must be at about the highest point in the cemetery," Duncan says, looking down the hill where we stand. Then, "There *is* such a thing as a Kansas sky—that bright blue, and those little white clouds . . ."

People begin arriving, a widow with her daughter, the doctor's wife (he has had a stroke and can't come), two men who worked at the mill for Graham thirty years ago. Introductions, identifi-cations.

"What really cracked me up," Duncan said later, "was how everyone was introducing you, 'This is Elizabeth Henley's daughter.' Not even Elizabeth Paulsen. They were really going way back."

Then the robed Episcopal minister is there, and Graham says to me, "Ellie? We're ready to start now." Dick tucks my arm into his and says, as we walk across the dry hillocks, "You've had some experience with this sort of thing, haven't you?"

The boys and I sit in the first row of folding chairs, and Graham, Jr., places Duncan next to me. The minister reads selections that Mavis, who remains exhausted in California, has requested. I stare at the little box of ashes and think, "Is that all?" Graham, Jr., next to me, raises his hand to his eyes several times. At the end, the American Legion Post Commander accepts a folded flag to be given by the family to the high school in Graham's memory.

The service is short. Then the "Thank you's" and "Good-bye's" mixed with "Hello's" to the late-comers. Duncan and I identify ourselves to the Post commander (Post No. 6). His name is Robert Riley, part of that endless family that lived near Grandmother's house. "Why—your father was our first post commander! We've got his picture on the wall down there with all the other commanders. Come down and see. We've got a brand new $375,000 building—all paid for. We serve lunches too. This is Friday. You could have fish or shrimp . . . "

Graham, Jr., meanwhile has an invitation for us from the doctor's wife to lunch at the country club. She says to me, "You don't know how bad Frank felt the day your grandfather died. Usually, he could accept those things, but that morning he just—came home—after he'd been up at the house." Grandfather died at ninety-two. The doctor had then been "the new young doctor," only a few years in Atchison.

A gray-haired man says to me, "Hello. I'm Mack McKinney."

"Oh—you were one of those bad McKinney boys who lived behind Graham and Mavis."

"I had a brother," he offers hopefully. "Donald."

"Oh—he was worse." Mack looks relieved.

A youngish couple presents themselves, and the man says, "I'm Bill Graham, Jr."

"My God! You look like Bill Graham, *Sr.*!" Great-uncle Will's grandson.

We arrange to meet at the club, and after more directions pick up Jen and the children. It is the same golf course where Grandfather went to work off his emotions after putting my parents and me on the train to move to St. Louis, and where Grandmother followed him crying, "They've taken my baby!"

He replied, "It's *their* life, Ellen. It's *their* life." Whap! at the golf ball.

We lunch at a big round table as various persons come to speak. A sweet-looking child, blond, jeaned, sexless, comes smiling to me saying, "I'm Andy Graham. My mom told me to come over." This is the *daughter* of Bill Graham, Jr., though we all guessed wrong on her gender.

I have brought some old pictures of Grandmother's house. Dick looks at one and says, almost with a child's glad recognition, "Why, there's Grandpa! That's a *good* picture of Grandpa!"

Graham and I are next to each other and have such an urge to talk that we must remember not to exclude the others. As we leave, he puts his arm around me and says, "It's strange how we come in and out of each other's lives—not very often, but when it's important."

Dick and Graham have a three o'clock plane out of Kansas City. We want to drive around town. They have already done so.

"The elms have all died," says Dick in a tone of betrayal. "Do you remember how they used to meet over the street?" and Graham says, "Everything looks so small."

We say our good-byes—and are on our own. I want to look

again, to find it all, but I am afraid that what *is* may obliterate what *was*. And what is it I hope to find? I can't say, exactly, but it is something very precious, something I want to believe existed once, even if it couldn't last.

I direct Duncan to Third Street and the right block. "Turn here." Slowly. "Stop."

"Here?"

"Here."

We park at the curb and look across the street. The house is green. (Mavis had her way at last. Subsequent owners must have repeated the color. Surely there has been another paint job in twenty-four years!) It looks a bit shabby. Some of the lattice under the porch has fallen in. Things aren't too bad, though the shrubs are overgrown, and Grandmother's flower beds are mostly gone. We have been told that five nuns now live in the house, that the parish rents it and houses some of its teachers there. Good. They'll be kind.

With the family strung out behind me on the sidewalk, I mount the porch stairs. I look for what I always looked for at first: the porch swing which my uncle Graham made in manual training. It is there! I am stunned. It is green now, but that's forgivable. It is still held up by the familiar rusty chains.

The built-in wooden seats that edged the porch railing are gone, as are the flower boxes. I ring the bell, not the old key-turn type in the center of the front door, but one by the side, pedestrian, push-button. But maybe it was there before. After all, how often did I ring the bell? It was Grandmother's house, and the door was always unlocked.

It is only then that I wonder for the first time if anyone is home. Someone was always at home in Grandmother's house. In a few moments, the door is opened by a pleasant-looking young woman in T-shirt and jeans. I explain (all our last names!) and ask if we may just walk around the yard.

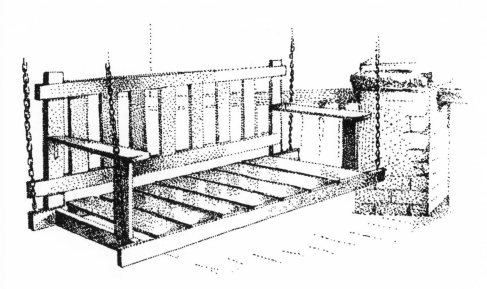

"Of course," she says. "In fact, come in. Just let me put my shoes on."

We enter the vestibule and are across it in less than a completed stride. Surely *that* was bigger? The nun (Sister Mary Mahoney) is in love with the house. "Look at the hardware," she says, turning the front door knob. I don't have to. We are in the front hall, and I am looking at the stairway.

"The Captain is still there," I say. They all look at me quizzically, the nun, my son and his wife, the children. "The Captain," I repeat. "See—this big newel post at the foot of the stairs was the captain, and his army was up the stairs behind him—all the posts in the bannister were his soldiers. And he was the good one. The other two round newel posts where the stairs turn were the heads of the two other armies, the bad ones. But even though there were more bad ones than good ones, the Captain always won."

"And the good one wore the big hat," murmurs the nun. She understands.

I look automatically up the staircase, as I always did, for the two silver-framed steel engravings. I know very well that Mother gave them to the doctor when she dismantled Grandmother's house. The doctor's wife confessed at the cemetery that she gave them later to a charity sale. ("They just didn't go with anything in our house.") I struggle to recall their titles. "Introducing the Bride," a picture story of a young woman being presented by a young man to a disapproving older woman was one. But the other? Something like "An Interrupted Courtship" of a young, courting couple disturbed by the entrance of a child. That one hung on the landing.

It is hard for me not to lead the way, I know it so well. Much is different, of course. Most of the woodwork has been painted white. But my memory has tricked me. One door, for some reason, has been left its original wood stain, which is darker than the golden oak finish that I remember.

The stained glass windows are gone, doubtless temporarily out of date and now desired and valuable. One used to be halfway up the staircase and one in the downstairs lavatory, an inclusion when the house was modernized. Having the stained glass in the lavatory made it possible to sit in privacy and look out of the different-colored pieces of glass at Great-grandmother Graham's house next door, making it seem to change colors. The nun smiles again. She is avid for information.

"You mean these are the original shutters?" in the library windows.

"Yes, and this is the window where you put the iceman's card, because it could be seen from the street."

"The iceman's card?"

I explain what this is—was. I am beginning to feel like an Original Source of Oral History.

There are changes and surprises. The tile in the front room fireplace is brown. I remembered it green. The old chandeliers, once gas but converted to electricity, have been replaced. There is carpeting on the floors, so the door from the library to the back porch won't open.

"It always stuck anyway," I say.

Of course, the wallpaper is different. The plate rail in the dining room seems much lower. I used to amuse myself at family meals when I was tired of listening to the grown-ups by looking at the plates propped on it at regular intervals, the grape-patterned, footed silver tray, the Royal Doulton "Cypress" plate in orange and blue, the wooden carved bread tray with "Gieb uns heute unsere täglich Brot" on it.

But there haven't been structural changes, no walls have been knocked out, no rooms rearranged. There is some water damage to window sills. Sister Mary asks Jen's advice on repairing them. "If you just put something into a good house, like this, it will last forever."

The kitchen has been somewhat modernized, but the old three-cornered broom closet is there, and the pantry, with the door removed. The wooden bannister on the back porch has been re-placed with metal, the wooden seat and the grape arbor are gone. We go to the basement, and I warn Jen about the steps before the door is even open. We go into the brick-paved laundry room, which I tell the nun is a very sunny room if she will just unboard the windows. She seems ready to do it now.

I want to see if it still says "Graham Henley Ofic" on the door to an inner room. The remnant of a day's play when my uncle was a boy, it is testimony to his permanent inability to spell. In his last letter to me, he wrote "embollism (sp?)." The door has been painted over.

"Do you remember which panel it was on? Maybe I could sand it down," the nun suggests gently.

"Oh—never mind."

All this time there is a smell of baking, quite proper for Grand-mother's house. With a gasp, the nun dashes for the kitchen to snatch a cake from the oven. Then she proudly displays the crooked back stairs, which Duncan and David discover is a "secret" way up. The stairs were once my secret.

The nun has my old room at the head of the front stairs, a room of many sides and angles. "Look," she shows us, "the old light fixtures with the side you turn on for gas and the other for elec-tricity." Of course. They were on either side of the bureau. A surprise: the half-circle window on the front wall, above the spot where the high headboard of the bed came, is brilliant stained glass. I had the former impression of something muted. The nun says there seems to have been a curtain rod there, and I remember a sort of white netting over the window.

We go every place except the attic. I would like to (the nun calls it "unique"), but I know it would be about a hundred and twenty degrees up there.

We walk around the yard. Again, my memory proves faulty: the back sidewalk is paved with large red sandstone slabs. It is the public sidewalk on Third Street that is the herringbone brick pat-tern.

"All of this long terrace here was flowers."

"It *was*?" I show her how the flower beds between this yard and Great-grandmother's were once double beds, facing both ways. She takes notes and says she wants to bring her students here to see what a Victorian house was like.

"You look like a Graham," she tells me. "You have Graham eyes. Do you know any of the Catholic Grahams?"

"I didn't know there were any." But Andy Graham, of the lunch table, was her student.

At last, feeling that we have taken up too much of Sister Mary's time, we say good-bye.

"If they ever want to get rid of the swing, I'll buy it. Don't let them chop it up for firewood."

"Oh, *no!* I won't."

Next door at Great-grandmother's house no one answers my ring. We have been told that the house has been bought by an "out-of-town millionaire who doesn't spend much time there and never asks anyone into his house." I call Jen onto the porch to see the stone balustrade and the big, shallow bird-bath-type dish on a pedestal. I remember it faintly with green plants trailing out of it. It is empty now.

We make a slow pilgrimage around town, depending on my memory and sense of direction. I can't find Miss Effie's house, where his wife waited out Lieutenant. Rowan's carrying the message to Garcia. Is it because I have forgotten the way, or has that suspicious-looking subdivision of new houses carpet-bagged the deep lawn with its big trees? We drive up the Orphan's Home road. The big, old central building is still there, surrounded by a scattering of small buildings. The sign at the entrance says "Atchison Youth Center." The hospital, new when Dick was born, now obviously takes itself very seriously, with all kinds of wings, therapy buildings and ancillary medical attachments. When, at age ten, I came to see Mavis after Dick's birth, she said, "Go into the nursery and see the baby, Ellen." And I went, unattended, into the room where the babies were, found him, and with one finger touched him on the left fist. When I told him that at lunch, he laughed and said, "And that's why I've always been left-handed."

We double over to Fifth Street to see Graham and Mavis's old house, the house where I was born. Grandfather had owned it then, renting it to my parents, for a minimal amount I'm sure, while my father re-established himself after their war. The old Childress house is still next door, but Childress' Grocery on the corner is now a drug store.

Back down Fourth Street, we pass the Mitchell house. It is still Victorian splendid and now houses the Atchison Historical Society. All of the Mitchells are now dead or moved away. I have heard that the family gave the house to the town.

And here, next to the new historical society, is the house which belonged to my Other Grandmother. It is unrecognizable. The front porch is gone, and the entrance has been moved from the center to the side. I try to imagine what changes have occurred inside. They must have combined the hall and living room to make one big, bright room, no longer shaded by the porch overhang. A child's tricycle lies upended on the top of the terrace. There is life in that house now.

Then we head for Commercial Street and the Legion Hall (Post No. 6). The bartender shows us the post commanders' pictures lining the corridor. Sure enough, there is my father in his World War I naval aviator's uniform, occupying the Number One position. I remember hearing that Col. Theodore Roosevelt, Jr., came out for the dedication of the post. He impressed Mother when he spent some time at their house and turned down the guest room bed-spread before taking a nap. She thought he had been well brought up. Duncan discovers that my father's first name is misspelled, and I determine to offer to pay for a new plaque.

Then we are on the blazing street again.

"I'm hungry!" This from David.

"We'll see if we can find a place where we can buy some ice cream." I am thinking of Gilbert's Ice Cream Parlor which used to be on Commercial Sreet, where they have now put the mall. I know it is gone, but as we wait for a WALK light (and *that*'s new in Atchison) I turn to a woman on the corner and ask if there is such a place. Yes, a drugstore in the next block. We tramp in, near collapse, and find—a soda fountain, where they *make* ice cream sodas! We clamber onto stools. A man in a workman's cap offers to move over so that Duncan can sit down. Chocolate ice cream sodas appear for those who wish them. Remembering Great-grandmother's "invention," a Lemon Smooth, served at John Kaff's Drug Store, I try for the closest substitute. They offer me a "Bubble-Up," a lemon drink which I don't know, and vanilla ice cream. Aided by a long spoon and nostalgia, I am satisfied.

On the way to the Legion Hall I saw the Presbyterian Church. I remember that there are memorial windows to my grandparents there. I direct Duncan back to it by the sight of spires in the sky. They turn out to be on the county courthouse. The church is another block over and doesn't reach so high. Across from it is the high school building which my grandfather, as a board of education member, helped to build.

"1908," Jen reads from the cornerstone. "In the city, people who used a school that old would say they were underprivileged." The building looks fine.

The church is locked, but we find an open side entrance.

"Hello?"

The church secretary is there, working on the bulletins. We go through the genealogical explanations again. She doesn't know *which* windows, but we may look at them all. We do. It is the church in which Grandmother played the organ and my parents were married.

David sits in a pew and asks Duncan to stand up in front and talk.

"What about?"

"Oh, *you* know. About God and things like that."

We see all of the church and Sunday School rooms. "We're sorry to interrupt your work."

"Oh, that's all right. It helps to break up the afternoon."

As the time for our flight approaches, we return to the motel for a final splash of water on our faces. We drive up the river road for a look at the Missouri. Then, back to the bridge. David yawns.

"Do you want to put your head in my lap?"

"I can't—because of the seat belt."

"Here—we'll release it, and I'll be your seat belt." He flops his head, complete with policeman's hat, which he has worn all day, into my lap and is asleep before we hit the Missouri side. Connie, on my other side, is intent upon "training" a fly. It rests on her finger. When it leaves, she says, "Come back," and it comes. (I suspect the remnants of her chocolate soda may influence its discipline.)

Duncan says suddenly, "You know what I liked best? The cemetery. That sounds morbid, but it wasn't."

"No. For me it was always a happy place."

"I felt comfortable in that little town," he muses. "I don't know why. I've never been there."

"Yes, you have. When you were a baby." Crawling on the porch floor, swinging in the swing with Grandfather.

"Oh—was I?—It's as if it were welcoming me. As if it were waiting for me."

"Yes."

"I felt as if I had found my roots." Silence. He tries again. "I had a feeling of—peace."

I am grateful. Grateful that he feels what I feel. I know, then, that it is real and there and lasting. Grandmother's house, with its sense of timelessness and calm, is still there for me and for him. And for his children, what heritage?

David slumbers in my lap.

Connie wants to take her fly onto the plane.

I leave that for Jen to handle.